Indo-European Noun Inflection:
A DEVELOPMENTAL HISTORY

Kenneth Shields, Jr.

Foreword by
William R. Schmalstieg

The Pennsylvania State University Press
University Park and London

Library of Congress Cataloging in Publication Data

Shields, Kenneth
  Indo-European noun inflection

Includes bibliography
        1. Proto-Indo-European language--Nominals.
        2. Proto-Indo-European language--Inflection.
        I. Title.
        P572.S53   415   82-467
        ISBN 0-271-00311-1   AACR2

Photo-ready copy by Mae Smith

Printed in the United States of America

For My Family

Contents

Foreword

Professor Shields' analysis of the Indo-European noun declension
is an admittedly speculative account based on a feeling that the
earliest forms of the common language were isolating in nature and
that only in the course of time did the language attain the inflectional endings present in the earliest attested sources. In Shields'
view, at the earliest stage of Indo-European the nominal classes
were divided into three semantic categories, viz. inanimate, animate,
and natural agent.

Making full use of older and more recent linguistic literature he
has tried to show how Indo-European may have passed from an ergative
language to a nominative-accusative language through the development
of an assonance concord relationship between a zero marked ergative
and a zero marked nonpersonal verbal suffix. Although this clearly
differs from my own views on the matter, I would quote from Paul
Feyerabend's book *Against Method* (London, 1978, p. 35), in which he
writes: 'Proliferation of theories is beneficial for science, while
uniformity impairs its critical power.'

Unfortunately, many Indo-Europeanists hold to the view that, since
case syncretism is attested, then it is not speculative to assume
case syncretism in the unattested evolution of Indo-European. But
there is a vast amount of unrecorded linguistic change, and I do
not see this lack cf data as any particular help in the creation of
a theory. Since case endings must have arisen during the evolution
of a language (unless, indeed, languages were born with them) it is
no more speculative to propose theories about the origin of case
endings than to propose theories about their loss. In fact, when
we are dealing with the unknown, all theories are to some extent
speculative and it is in the nature of the abductive process that
some persons will be more impressed by one analogy and others more
impressed by another. *No two situations are ever exactly alike,*
so scholar A may be impressed by the differences between the evolutionary developments of two languages, whereas scholar B may be

impressed by the similarities. If the facts forced the interpretation, it would be difficult to see how there could ever be any dis-
agreement about anything.

An argument could be made that it would be wise to reject all
scientific theories because, as Feyerabend states (op. cit., p. 65):
'The demand to admit only those theories which are consistent with
the available and accepted facts . . . leaves us without any theory
. . . for there is not a single theory that is not in some trouble
or other.'

The human being, however, is infinitely curious to learn about
his own nature, and attempts to enlighten him are among the proudest
achievements of the human race. Thus another imaginative attempt
to make some sense out of the maze of data which the Indo-European
languages present is to be welcomed on the market place.

William R. Schmalstieg

Acknowledgements

I wish to take this opportunity to express my heartfelt gratitude
to Professor William Schmalstieg, without whose inspiration, advice,
and encouragement this book would not have been written. During
the past decade it has been my pleasure to know Bill Schmalstieg as
a teacher, as a scholar, and, most importantly, as a friend. I also
want to thank Professor Philip Baldi for his helpful suggestions.
I am sure, however, that neither one of these fine Indo-Europeanists
would agree completely with what I say in this volume. Finally, I
am sincerely grateful to Millersville State College for its generous
support of this project.

                                    Kenneth C. Shields, Jr.

Lancaster, Pennsylvania

1 Introduction

1. The purpose of this volume, strangely enough, is not to convince
the reader of the unqualified validity of the specific analyses presented. Indeed, I freely admit that nearly everything I say here
cannot be proven absolutely correct. Rather, its purpose is to demonstrate, on the basis of some interesting new proposals about the
structure of natural language and its evolution and about the structure and the evolution of the Indo-European language, as well as on
the basis of some more traditional proposals about these matters,
that the Indo-European language (specifically, its system of nominal
inflection) and the evolution it underwent from its earliest stages
to the appearance of the individual dialects may have been very different from what is generally assumed. I am sure that many will
dismiss what I say as mere speculation since attempts at theoriza-
tion which deals with the primitive origins of various linguistic
phenomena have been shunned by many contemporary scholars. In this
regard I am reminded of Fowler's assessment (1957: 54) of Gonda's
book *The Character of the Indo-European Moods* (1956): "The ultimate
question raised by Gonda's book, and one which will be raised by all
other books written in a similar way on similar subjects, is whether
it is useful to ask questions about 'original meaning'. In 1956
[and apparently in 1980--K.S.] the answer must surely be that, if
one is to avoid argument over mere differences of opinion, the search
for original meanings had better, for the time being, be postponed.
In the absence of a new method which will allow a more exact extrap-
olation, it is at least doubtful whether any one person can do more
than interpret in terms of his own theory evidence of such extreme
complexity as is now available for examination. . . . It is difficult, therefore, to understand how more can profitably be said on
this or on similar subjects until some distributional trends have
been accurately plotted in all the related languages in which evidence is to be found." Fowler's attitude is exemplary of the one
which is widely held concerning the reconstruction of what Lehmann

(1958: 182) terms "Pre-Indo-European." However, I believe that this
attitude is a result of taste rather than substance. Most of historical and comparative linguistic theory fails to embody the large
measure of certainty which Fowler seems to ascribe to it. How many
"differences of opinion" exist regarding the origin of the Germanic
dental preterite, the Italo-Celtic genitive singular suffix $-\bar{\imath}$, or
the Standard English third person verbal ending $-s$ (cf. Shields
1980a), even though substantial and thoroughly analyzed data about
these formations exist? It seems to me that when someone asserts
that the reconstruction of Pre-Indo-European is "speculative" in comparison to the reconstruction of Proto-Indo-European, Proto-Germanic,
or Proto-Romance, he is actually referring to a meager difference in
degree, not a difference in kind. My reconstructions will be viewed
as speculative in another sense as well: as I have pointed out,
they deviate significantly from traditional notions about early Indo-
European, although these traditional notions themselves are frequently regarded as speculative; and because they look strange, they will
naturally be considered suspect. But this deviation does not mean
that I have ignored what is known about the structure and the evolution of language in general and the Indo-European language in particular, or that I have rejected the traditional methods of linguistic
reconstruction; instead, I have merely looked at the old data in the
light of what I consider to be advances in the theory of language
(Indo-European and otherwise) structure and change. In other words,
in this monograph I am speculating about the Indo-European language
in the true sense of the word. I maintain that speculation in this
sense is not an unscientific exercise but is instead the essence of
creativity through which progress in any field is made. That "idle
speculation" can indeed further understanding is easily demonstrated,
ironically enough, by an example from the history of Indo-European
studies: the Neogrammarian Movement itself was born in a furor about
the "wild" ideas of non-traditionalists like Brugmann, Osthoff, and
Delbrück. Therefore, although many scholars will not find what I say
here to appeal to their tastes, I submit that my arguments are sound
from the point of view of current knowledge about matters linguistic.

1.1   Reconstruction. As the preceding remarks indicate, I believe
that there are very few unique solutions to the problems posed by
historical and comparative linguistics. However, this belief does
not mean that I am advocating the idea that any reconstruction is as
good as another. Reconstructions which are based on incomplete data,
i.e. data taken from only a subset of daughter languages, or which
violate structural or evolutionary constraints on natural languages

are obviously not as valid as reconstructions which are based on complete data and are typologically sound. But because so little is known about such matters as what really constitutes complete evidence and what the structural constraints on languages are, it is difficult to evaluate alternative reconstructions. Often times a linguist cannot be sure whether a particular construction attested in just two or three daughter languages is a relic formation or an innovation which developed in an independent but parallel manner in each; and, as Schmalstieg (1980: 17) points out, "The problem with universals . . . is [that--K.S.] . . . there seems to be no adequate method of distinguishing accidental universals from necessary universals. If, for example, we divide the world's languages up into the types, agglutinative, synthetic and isolating, we may have a general view of the possible types of languages. But suppose as a result of some cataclysm all of the speakers of one of the types of these languages were wiped out. A future investigator with no knowledge of the historical situation might declare that languages of the type spoken by the eliminated population were impossible." Thus, although one can say, for example, that a reconstruction of Indo-European which considers Hittite, Tocharian, and Celtic data is superior to one that does not, there are still many possible reconstructions of the language, each being of equal merit.

Pessimistic as it sounds, although new knowledge can help the historical linguist better evaluate reconstructions, I believe that no amount of new knowledge will ever permit him to assert the reality of reconstructions because the methods of reconstruction themselves are faulty. This is the thrust of Pulgram's criticism (1959, 1961) of what has come to be called the "realist" view of reconstructions, cf. Wyatt 1972: 688. Pulgram (1959: 422-423) says: ". . . it must be conceded that . . . a reconstruction is something of a fiction, since 'the terms *Proto-*, *Ur-*, *Primitive* are firmly attached to formulae which are timeless, non-dialectal, and non-phonetic' [(Twadell 1948: 139)--K.S.]. Anything in linguistics that is timeless, non-dialectal, and non-phonetic, by definition does not represent a real language. That is to say, the uniformity which reconstructed Proto-Indo-European exhibits is not representative of reality." In Shields 1980b, I try to support this claim further by demonstrating, on the basis of Gimbutas' identification (1970, 1973, 1974) of the Kurgan Culture as Indo-European, that there existed significant sociolinguistic variation within the Indo-European speech community. Because the precise nature and scope of this variation lies beyond the methods of linguistic reconstruction, it must be assumed that reconstructed Proto-Indo-European is not a real language, but rather an abstract linguistic construct--the position held by the "formulists," cf.

Wyatt 1972: 688. As long as no definitive reconstruction can be made because the methods of reconstruction "lose information," it would seem that unresolved issues of analysis will remain. As a result of such unresolved problems, scholars often make choices among competing reconstructions on the basis of unscientific criteria, even though they are reluctant to admit this fact. That a similar situation exists in contemporary theoretical linguistics is emphasized by Schane (1976: 184): "Due to the nature of the internal or the external evidence at hand, there is no 'logical' reason to prefer one analysis to the other. It is for this reason that the choice may be entirely an esthetic one. . . . Although there may be many types of arguments around, I conclude that there are few good ones and even fewer convincing ones. For the moment, the best argument, like beauty, is in the mind of the beholder." In what follows, I shall at times state a preference for one scholar's reconstruction over that of another on the basis of my esthetic sensibilities alone; but I fully recognize that my choice is not predicated on any substantive evidence and that, objectively, the alternative reconstruction has as much validity as the one I subjectively find more satisfactory. It is my hope that the reconstructions which I posit here will be viewed in the same way by those who find alternative explanations more to their liking.

1.2   Summary. My focus is on the development of Indo-European nominal inflection, although, by necessity, some consideration is given to morphological and syntactic patterns of other parts of speech. The body of the text is divided into three main chapters. Chapter 2, *Nominal Inflection in Early Indo-European*, traces the development of a nominative-accusative system in Indo-European from an earlier ergative system. The chapter includes subsidiary discussions of the origin of grammatical gender, the origin of the differing inflectional patterns of neuter nouns (i.e. the fact that some form a nominative-accusative in *-∅, others in *-N [= m or n]), and the origin of the -r-/-n-stem nouns. In Chapter 3, *The Enrichment of the Case System*, I consider the emergence of an oblique case from an earlier objective case in *-N through the appearance of certain inflectional elements (*-s, *-i, *-T [= t or d], and *-bh). The bifurcation of this oblique case into still other cases, the emergence of an autonomous vocative case from an earlier nominative-vocative case, the nature of the concordial system, and the appearance of the nominative suffix *-s are also taken up here. Chapter 4, *The Origin of the Non-Singular and the Development of the Feminine Gender*, considers both of these inflectional categories and demonstrates their close etymological relationship. The Germanic weak adjectival de-

4

clension is then analyzed as a formation intimately related to these
two categories. Chapter 4 concludes with a discussion of the origin
of the endingless locative in order to demonstrate the far-reaching
implications of the analyses presented in this monograph. Chapter 5
is a chronological summary of the linguistic changes discussed
throughout the book.

1.3   Method. As I have already indicated, my reconstructions of
Indo-European are based on the traditional methods of comparative
and internal reconstruction. Moreover, I posit no new processes of
linguistic change but, instead, utilize in my explanations of the
evolution of Indo-European the established means by which languages
alter their structure. What makes my reconstructions seem so radi-
cally different from the ones generally seen in comparative grammars
is that I subscribe to some very recent proposals about language
change and the structure of Indo-European, and that I believe certain
traditional processes of change are far more important in the development of Indo-European (and perhaps all languages) than many historical linguists do. At this point, a brief discussion concerning
the assumptions which underlie my analyses seems to be in order.

1.3.1 Language Variation and Language Change. Traditional views
about language evolution have been greatly altered in the last few
years because of the findings of variation theory, pioneered by
Weinreich, Labov, and Herzog (1968). However, Indo-European studies,
with few exceptions,[1] have remained largely unaffected by these important discoveries. In this monograph I attempt to apply a number
of the ideas of the so-called sociolinguistic school to the structural development of the Indo-European language. The key concept of
all variation theory is the *variable rule*, which is employed to
account for the fact that linguistic change "begins variably rather
than categorically; that is, it begins as a rule that sometimes operates and sometimes does not" (Bailey 1973: 157). Although much of
the research in variation theory has dealt with phonology, it is
clear that changes at other levels of language follow the same patterns (Bailey 1973: 164). Reighard (1974: 251) succinctly summar-
izes the basic ideas of this approach to language evolution: ". . .
there are at least three dimensions through which a change . . . can
expand and evolve. There can be phonological [and other types of--
K.S.] evolution, when the probability of application of a variable
rule, or the relative importance of some part of its environment,
increases gradually to a point where the rule becomes categorical
(obligatory). There can be demographic evolution, when the rule
spreads through the population of speakers of the language either in

time or in space (cf. the many cases where the increase in probability of application of a rule is a function of age in a given population, or the geographical spread of many attested changes in the
literature). And finally there can be lexical evolution when a
change spreads progressively through the lexicon of a language,
applying first to a few words, later to a group, and finally to the
whole lexicon. Here, Labov [(1972)--K.S.] distinguishes two kinds
of lexical spread. *Ordered decomposition* is when the phonological
evolution of the rule itself determines the expanding subset of lexical items to which it can apply. . . . The second kind of lexical
spread is *random decomposition* where the rule appears to apply in a
haphazard manner to some subset of all phonological forms to which
it could apply, or alternatively, applies to some phonologically
well-defined class of forms but in addition to a few others which
appear to be included by exception, as it were." In phonology this
concept of random decomposition is central in understanding another
important idea of the variationists--residue. Chen and Wang (1975:
256) explain: "A phonological rule gradually extends its scope of
operation to a larger and larger portion of the lexicon, until all
relevant items have been transformed by the process. A phonological
innovation may turn out to be ultimately regular, i.e. to affect
all relevant lexical items, given the time to complete its course.
But more often than linguists have thought, a phonological rule
peters out toward the end of its life span, or it is thwarted by
another rule competing for the same lexemes." The unaffected items
are called *residue*, and they simply represent exceptions to sound
changes. All in all, then, I shall assume that linguistic evolution
is an inherently gradual and variable process, with the lexical
items or the morphological and syntactic patterns which are under-
going a change "fluctuating either randomly or according to some
such factor as tempo or style" between the old and the innovative
form or pattern during the earlier stages of that change (Wang 1969:
15). As time passes, a change spreads throughout the lexicon (or to
all relevant environments if it is morphological or syntactic) until
it becomes completely generalized or it "peters out."

1.3.2 Indo-European Monophthongizations. Schmalstieg (1973, 1974c,
1980: 21-45) has argued that "within the development of Indo-European
there took place a monophthongization" of various preconsonantal
diphthongs "at least for word-final position" (1973: 101). The
changes included the following:

Original Form	Prevocalic Form	Preconsonantal Form
*-ow	*-ow	*-ō
*-oy	*-oy	*-ē
*-ew	*-ew	*-ū
*-ey	*-ey	*-ī
*-ay	*-ay	*-ā
*-aw	*-aw	*-ō
*-ir	*-ir	*-ī
*-iN (N = m or n)	*-iN	*-ī
*-er	*-er	*-ē
*-eN	*-eN	*-ē
*-ar	*-ar	*-ā
*-aN	*-aN	*-ā
*-or	*-or	*-ō
*-oN	*-oN	*-ō
*-ur	*-ur	*-ū
*-uN	*-uN	*-ū

Of course, this proposal is a controversial one; and it has not es-
caped criticism, cf. Pajares 1976: 162-171. But Schmalstieg (1978)
has refuted Pajares' arguments against the hypothesis and has thereby demonstrated that his theory of monophthongization at least lies
within the realm of distinct possibility. Although the proposal
cannot be proven absolutely correct, I find it to be a satisfying
explanation of the data and will assume its validity in what follows.

Schmalstieg has presented a great deal of material in support of
his theory, so I shall mention only a few supporting examples here.
Since a number of monophthongizations will be especially important
in later chapters, my comments will be limited to them.

In support of the claim that *-VN became *-V̄, Schmalstieg (1974c:
187) says: "The Indo-European 1st sg. secondary ending *-om and the
primary ending *-ō (derived from *-om in pre-consonantal sandhi) were
originally merely sandhi variants, see Szemerényi, 1970, 308. In
general the phonologically newer form in *-ō takes over the primary
function of the present tense, whereas the older form, the ending
*-om is found in the non-present formations. Thus, for example, we
find the 1st sg. pres. Gk. phérō, Skt. bhár-ā-mi vs. the 1st sg. imperfect Gk. épher-on, Skt. ábhar-am." This same sound change is
also responsible for the fact that "ancient Greek has the noun dô
(< *dom) vs. the more common thematic form dómos" (1974c: 188).
Likewise, "The Skt. nom. sg. vr̥tra-hā (< *ghʷen) shows a stem alternate with final -n in the other cases, e.g., acc. sg. vr̥tra-han-am,
instr. sg. vr̥tra-ghn-ā, dat. sg. vr̥tra-ghn-e, abl.-gen. sg. vr̥tra-
ghn-aḥ, loc. sg. vr̥tra-haṇi, -ghni, voc. sg. vr̥tra-han. The nomina-

tive singular shows the pre-consonantal sandhi, i.e. $-\bar{a} < *-\bar{e} < **-eN$, whereas the vocative singular shows the pre-vocalic sandhi, i.e. $-an < *-eN < **-eN$" (1974c: 187). Schmalstieg (1973: 107-108) provides the following examples of the passage of $*-ey$ to $*-\bar{\imath}$ and of $*-oy$ to $*-\bar{e}$: "The elementary form $*bhe$ 'to be, to become' could have taken the suffix $-y$ to create the morpheme $*bhe-y > *bh\bar{\imath}$ in pre-consonantal sandhi position. The form $*bh\bar{\imath}$ is reflected in Lat. $f\bar{\imath}-s$, fit 'becomes, is made', Gk. $ph\hat{\imath}tu$ 'shoot, scion', OCS $bi-m\breve{\upsilon}$ 'I would be'. Perhaps Old English $b\bar{e}o$, $b\bar{\imath}o$ belong here also. Forms such as Lith. $-bite$, $-bime$ are to be added here also. The short vowel of such forms is due to their use in enclitic position according to Stang, 1966, 429 . . . . The form $*bho-y$ in pre-consonantal position is attested in the OCS third singular imperfect form $b\breve{e}$ and perhaps in the Old Prussian preterit $b\bar{e}i = /b\bar{e}/$, both of which forms reflect Indo-European $*bh\bar{e}$." Similarly, "The Indo-European root for 'to drink' seems to have been $*pe-$ or $*po-$ variously suffixed with $-y$ or $-w$. The form $*p\bar{\imath}-$ ($< *pe-y$) in pre-consonantal position lives on in Slavic $piti$ 'to drink', Gk. $p\hat{\imath}n\bar{o}$ 'I drink' (with the imperative $p\hat{\imath}thi$ according to Frisk, 1970, 540), Skt. $p\bar{\imath}t\acute{a}$ 'drunk, sucked' and $p\bar{\imath}t\acute{\imath}$ 'drinking, a draught'. The $-y-$ element may also be present in the reduplicative syllable of Latin $bibit$ 'drinks'. The form $*po-y$ is apparently only found in such causatives as Slavic $po[j]iti$ 'to give to drink, to cause to drink'. The Sanskrit causative stem $p\bar{a}y-$ shows a phenomenon we shall see over and over again in this language. $*po-y$ in pre-consonantal position passed to $*p\bar{e}-$, a form attested in Skt. $p\bar{a}ti$ 'drinks', but in pre-vocalic position $*po-y$ should be represented by Skt. $*pay-$. What we actually find, however, is a contamination of the pre-vocalic and the pre-consonantal forms of this morpheme, i.e. $*p\bar{a}y$, a form with the length of the pre-consonantal form and with the $-y$ from the pre-vocalic form" (1973: 108).

As the first example clearly shows, sandhi doublets can be morphologized, with each variant assuming a particular function. That this process is not a terribly uncommon one is demonstrated by the fact that a parallel development is found in the history of English. "According to Strang, 1970, 262, the genitive singular of the first person pronoun /mi:n/ developed a form without final consonant for use before consonants. She writes: 'The alternative, my, min, provided the formal contrast which was later exploited grammatically, i.e., to distinguish possessive adjectives from pronouns'" (Schmalstieg 1977b: 126). "A somewhat similar example from the history of Estonian is quoted by Anttila, 1972, 79: 'In the beginning of the seventeenth century, the final $-n$ was about to disappear everywhere, but it was still retained if the following word began with a vowel. From such positions it could be generalized back into every position

in the first person singular, partly (presumably) to avoid homonymy
with the imperative *kanna* 'carry''" (Schmalstieg 1977b: 126).

1.3.3 Analogy. Like many historical linguists, I believe that
analogy plays a very important role in language change. Analogy is
usually thought of in terms of clearly defined proportions; but, as
Anttila (1972: 91-92) emphasizes, "Proportional analogy is only one
kind of analogy. Often proportions do not exist. . . . Strong evidence against the necessity of proportional analogy are forms where
the older shape is just covered over by new material without being
replaced in toto. Thus the expected plural of *cow*, *'ki'* [kai], was
adapted to the pattern of its antonym *ox* by the addition of the
plural marker *n*: [kai-n] *kine*. The old plural still lurks in the
word. . . . In German the past passive participles have a prefix *ge-*
(e.g., *ge-mach-t* 'made'). A verb like *essen* fused *ge-essen* into
gessen. The resulting form was deviant, as it seemed to lack the
syllable *ge-*; it was consequently supplied with it again, giving *ge-
gessen*, the current form." I believe that non-proportional analogy
is a very significant means of linguistic evolution since language
change is largely based on abductive reasoning, cf. Andersen 1973.
In the chapters which follow, I shall make frequent references to
two manifestations of non-proportional analogy—reinterpretation
(reanalysis) and contamination—because they seem to have been prime
motivators of change in Indo-European. In regard to reinterpretation, Anttila (1973: 8) notes that "surface ambiguity" is the situation that generally precipitates this analogical process. He says:
"A clear traditional example of the . . . [process of reinterpreta-
tion--K.S.] is the following from the history of Finnish. At the
time of the final *-m*'s we had sentences of the type:

näe	-	*m*	*poja*	-	*m*	*mene*	-	*vä*	-	*m*
see		I	boy		acc.	go		ing		acc.

'I see the boy go'

where the participle agrees in number and case with its head (*boy*).
Then final *-m*'s were replaced by *-n*'s through sound change and we
get a sentence *Näen pojan menevän*, where the previous grammatical
rules operate as well as before. Now, however, the surface is ambiguous, because the accusative merged in form with the genitive *pojan*
'of the boy'. And indeed, somebody reinterpreted this accusative as
a genitive. This is an abduction that would not show anywhere as
long as the original distribution is not transgressed. The abduction
surfaces in the new plural, which takes on deductively the genitive:

näen	*poik*	-	*i*	-	*en*	*menevän*
I see	boy		pl.		gen.	go

9

for the old *Näen pojat manevät*. . . . The participle has thereby cut
loose from the paradigm and become an uninflected infinitival form"
(1973: 8-9). Likewise, "English has synchronic ambiguity in cases
like *a name* vs. *an aim*, because they can be phonetically alike. In
the history of the language, there are cases where such an *n* (either
part of the article or other pronouns or the initial of a noun) has
been interpreted the wrong way. Old English *efeta* gave ME *evete*,
which ends up as NE *eft*. The current normal shape, however, was reanalyzed from *anevete* → *a-nevete*, giving *newt*. Similarly, Middle
English *eke-name* 'additional name' (compare to *eke* out a living) in-
corporated the *n* from the article, *anekename*, ending up as *nickname*
. . . . The reverse has happened to OE *nafugār* → *auger*, *napron* →
apron (compare *napery* 'linen' and *napkin*), and also in *adder* from ME
naddere (compare German *Natter*)" (Anttila 1972: 93-94). It would
seem that such reanalyses may even occur when surface ambiguity is
minimal. "Latin had a suffix *-nus* (e.g., *domi-nus* 'master' and
fāgi-nus 'of beech'). Applied to *ā*-stems, we get forms like *Rōmā-
nus* and *silvā-nus* 'forest deity'. At some point these were analyzed
as *Rōm-ānus* and *silv-ānus*, because new derivations were formed with
a suffix *-ānus* on stems without *ā*, for example, *mundānus* 'of the
world' (*mund-*), *urbānus* 'of the city' (*urb-*), and *montānus* 'of the
mountains' (*mont-*)" (Anttila 1972: 94). Antilla (1973: 10) notes
that although "the linguistic literature is full" of such changes,
they have generally been played down in importance because they are
difficult to assimilate into existing theories of language evolution.

Of course, contamination is simply morphological or lexical assimilation of two forms in the same semantic field, cf. Anttila 1972:
76. For example, "The influence of synonyms is exemplified by Finnish *viipale* 'slice', replaced by *siipale* after *siivu*, also 'slice'"
(Anttila 1972: 76). The operation of contamination in the evolution
of the Indo-European language has been recognized. Thus, in the system of verb endings, "Für die Aktiv-Reihe bekommen wir in der ein-
fachsten Form, den sogenannten Sekundär-Endungen, im Singular in der
1. Person *-m*, in der 2. *-s*, in der 3. *-t*. Die Endungen des
Präsens, die Primär-Endungen *-mi/*-si/*-ti*, unterscheiden sich von
dieser Reihe nur durch ein *-i*, das heute üblicherweise als eine
diektische Partikel zur Bezeichnung des 'Jetzt' erklärt wird. Auf
jeden Fall sind diese beiden Ausprägungen der Aktiv-Reihe genau parallel und weisen damit auf gemeinsamen Ursprung" (Seebold 1971: 189).
Likewise, Burrow (1973: 307) says about the Sanskrit first person
singular thematic verbal suffix *-āmi*: "This ending [*-mi*--K.S.] was
originally confined to the non-thematic classes, and a different
ending *-ō*. . . appeared in the thematic classes: Gk. *phérō*, Lat.
fero, Goth. *baíra*. Some such forms are preserved in Iranian (Av.

spasyā : Lat. *specio*), but usually in Iranian, and always in Sanskrit, *mi* from the non-thematic verbs is added to the older form: Skt. *bharāmi*, Av. *barāmi*." Finally, Safarewicz (1974: 48) maintains that "the middle-voice endings in Greek [*-mai*, *-sai*, *-tai*--K.S.] contain the consonants *-m-*, *-s-*, *-t-* which apparently have been introduced there from the active voice. Besides, the diphthong *ai* is here generalized." As these examples demonstrate, contamination can be a very functional process since it can serve to hypercharacterize forms. Malkiel (1957: 79) explains: "If a given linguistic formation develops in such a way as to allow, at a certain point, one of its distinctive features to stand out more sharply than at the immediately preceding stage, one may speak of hypercharacterization (or hyperdetermination) of that feature, in the diachronic perspective."

1.4   Case and Gender. As a final comment in this introduction, I wish to point out a problem which a study of this type automatically inherits--the ambiguity of the terms *case* and *gender*.

In one sense, *case* refers to the surface forms, or overt morphological markers, utilized as exponents of various syntactic functions. In other words, the nominative case in a given language is characterized by a set of one or more affixes. On the other hand, *case* may refer to the functions themselves, i.e., it may be used in reference to deep syntactic categories. Thus, the term *nominative case* may be a synonym for *agent*, *subject*, or the like. For the sake of simplicity, I shall also use the term *case* and its subcategories in both of these ways; but I shall be careful to specify whether I am referring to a formal entity or to a functional one.

Gender also shows an ambiguity, since sometimes it is described as a formal category, more precisely termed *grammatical gender*, and other times it is described as a notional category, more precisely termed *natural gender*. However, as Lyons (1971: 284) notes, gender classification in all languages, even in those where it is primarily formal in nature, has some semantic motivation. Therefore, the ambiguity of the word is an important aspect of its meaning. The fact that gender systems can evolve from being primarily formal in structure to being notional in structure and vice versa also justifies the use of the term *gender* in both senses.

NOTE

[1]See, e.g., Shields 1979b, 1980d, Forthcoming b.

2 Nominal Inflection in Early Indo-European

2.1   Earliest Indo-European. In its most primitive stages, Indo-European was probably an isolating language like Chinese. The validity of this hypothesis was recognized at the beginning of this century by Wheeler (1898: 538), who writes: "The compounds represent in their type survivals from a period in the history of the I.E. language before case endings became definitely affixed to the noun-'stems', and before grammatical gender was introduced; *akropólis* (and not *akrápolis*), *logopoiós* (not *logompoiós*), for instance, present on the one hand an adjective without concord, on the other a noun without case-ending (accus.). The noun-'stem' appears here, not as a grammatical abstraction, but as a petrified fact. . . ."
Similarly, Biese (1950: 3) remarks: "It is mostly assumed that the early history of Common Indo-European, a highly inflectional language, goes back into a non- inflectional or pre-inflectional stage, inflection in the form in which we find it in Common Ie. being of comparatively late development." Through various processes of evolution, the Indo-European language only gradually developed into the highly inflectional language that is reconstructed for the period just before the split of the main body of the Indo-European speech community.

Specht (1947: 353) expresses this same view of gradual development in regard to the case system when he observes: "Die Zahl der nachweisbaren 7 oder 8 idg. Kasus ist sicher nicht auf einmal entstanden, sondern sie ist allmählich ausgebaut worden." Lehmann (1958: 182-183) also subscribes to this position: "The cases expressing adverbial relationships (instrumental, dative, ablative, locative, and the genitive in some uses) are late: their endings differ from dialect to dialect; the plural endings for these cases are not attested in Hittite. . . . The development of the adverbial cases belongs then to the study of late Proto-Indo-European and the individual dialects."

Not only did the syntactic category of case develop only gradually, but the category of number also shows the same slow evolution. Thus, Hirt (1934: 23) says: "Eine besondere flektierte Form für den Plural war demnach ursprünglich nicht notwendig." He believes that a number of dialectal phenomena support this conclusion. For example, "Die neutralen *i*-Stämme gebrauchen als Plural im Aind. den Singular. *aprati̇́, asthū̇ri̇́, jāmi̇́, bhū̇ri, śámi, surabhi̇́, máhi* (AV.)" (1934:24). Likewise, "In diesem Fall haben wir auch zwei Fälle im Europäischen, nämlich 1. *tot* und *quot*. Vgl. *tot tam valida oppida, quot calamitates*" (Hirt 1934: 24). The structural identity of various neuter singular and non-singular forms in other stem-classes in Vedic Sanskrit (*ū̇́dhar* 'udder', *vásu* 'possession', *purú* 'league', *sā́nu* 'summit, top'), Homeric Greek (*hē̂mar* 'day'), and perhaps Hittite (*wetar* 'water', *uttar* 'thing', *zankilatar* 'punishment') further demonstrates that number distinctions emerged at a late date.[1] Lehmann (1974: 201-202) also writes: "The system of verb endings clearly points to an earlier period in which there was no verbal inflection for number. . . . For the dual and plural endings are obviously defective. We cannot reconstruct endings in these two numbers which are as well supported as are those of the singular, except for the third plural. . . . The number system is defective in substantival as well as in verbal inflection. The personal pronouns never did introduce expressions for plurality, as suppletive paradigms indicate, e.g., Hitt. *uk* 'I', *ueš̆* 'we', etc., in contrast with demonstratives, e.g., *kā̆š̆, kē̆* 'this, these', and nouns, e.g., *antuhš̆aš̆, antuhš̆eš̆* 'man, men'. . . . Number accordingly was not consistently applied in late PIE and the early dialects in accordance with natural reference. Subsequently application became more regular, and number congruence was carried out for both substantives and verbs." It is interesting to note in regard to the development of the number category that Hittite shows a lack of definitive number specification in the genitive endings *-aš̆* and *-an*. Kronasser (1956: 104) thus says: "Eine Eigentümlichkeit des Heth. ist es, dass der Plural keine voll ausgebildete Flexion aufweist und z.T. die Endungen des sg. verwendet, wie umgekehrt der g. pl. *-an* im sg. vorkommen kann (*Labarnan*)." Likewise, in the genitive plural "die lebendige paradigmatische Endung im Heth. ist jedoch *-as* (auch im Hh. *-ăs*), die mit der des g. sg. identisch ist" (Kronasser 1956: 105). The Hittite genitive suffix *-aš̆* is obviously cognate with the genitive-ablative singular suffix *-(e/o)s* reconstructed for the other Indo-European languages, while Hitt. *-an* "geht auf *-ōm* [i.e. *-ŏN--K.S.] züruck, das bei allen Stammklassen üblich war: [Gk. gen. pl.--K.S.] *podō̂n*, ai. *padā́m*, lat. *pedum*, [Gk.--K.S.] *lúkōn* u.a." (Kronasser 1956: 105). What this attested situation implies is that at one stage in its development, Indo-European had two genitive markers which were undifferentiated in terms of their num-

ber specification because the non-singular had not yet emerged as a
morphologically autonomous entity. That is, one can see here an
example of what Wandruszka (1969: 218) identifies as "paradigmatische
Polymorphie," "die Tatsache, dass in einer Sprache immer wieder ver-
schiedene [inflectional--K.S.] Formen für dieselbe Funktion verwendet
werden." As Wandruszka (1969) indicates, this property of natural
languages is surely a common one. For example, "Im Deutschen ist
die Funktion, den Plural eines Substantivs zu kennzeichnen, verschiedenen Formen anvertraut: *der Vater—die Väter, der Kater—die
Kater, der Vetter—die Vettern, der Retter—die Retter, das Brett—
die Bretter, das Bett—die Betten, das Fett—die Fette. . . .* Die
ursprüngliche Motivation dieser Polymorphie ist längst erloschen"
(Wandruszka 1969: 218-219).

The category of gender similarly evolved in a gradual manner, for
the emergence of a definitively feminine gender was a rather late
development in Indo-European. The early gender system was realized
morphologically in the opposition between an animate nominal class
and an inanimate (neuter) one. As Szemerényi (1970: 143) says:
"Das idg. System der drei Geschlechter muss aber aus einem Zwei-
klassensystem entstanden sein. Darauf weist allein schon die Tatsache, dass in altertümlichen Flexionsklassen das Mask. und Fem.
sich in der Flexion nicht unterscheiden, dagegen sich gemeinsam von
Neutrum abheben, vgl. z.B. [Gk.--K.S.] *patér, métēr.*" I believe
that this binary system continues to be preserved in Hittite (and
Luwian), where there appear "nur ein Genus commune (für das Mask.
und Fem.) und ein Neutrum" (Szemerényi 1970: 143). The hypothesis
that the Anatolian gender system is archaic has been strengthened
recently by the research of Brosman (1976, 1978). After examining
"the Hittite gender of the Indo-European feminines attested in that
language, in particular of those with inanimate referents," he concludes "that the evidence . . . does not accord well with the theory
of a lost feminine," since there appears to exist a connection between the Indo-European feminine and the Hittite neuter, not the
Hittite common gender as the loss of the feminine in Anatolian would
logically entail (1976: 143-144). This conclusion is also implied
by the data presented in "a similar survey of the Hittite cognates
of Proto-Indo-European neuters" (Brosman 1978: 94). Brosman (1978:
102-103) says: "Addition of the evidence concerning the neuters
reinforces the impression produced previously by consideration of
the feminines. The most obvious aspect of the new material is the
complete consistency with which the Indo-European neuters retained
their inherited gender throughout the period preceding the attesta-
tion of Hittite, which indicates that the vagaries of unknown early
analogies are not a sufficient explanation for the failure of the

14

forms presumed to have been original feminines to appear in the
Hittite common gender. That the number of precise cognates among
the neuters was two and a half times that found in the case of the
feminines is also noteworthy and is consistent with the view that
the neuter seems more likely than the feminine to have been in existence at the time of the separation of Anatolian. A further indication that what is reflected here is a declensional system consider-
ably earlier than that immediately reconstructible from comparison
of the traditional Indo-European languages is the fact that nine of
the fifteen neuters having Hittite cognates belonged to the *r/n-*,
consonant-, or *i*-stems. However, every class of Indo-European neuter was represented (unless one include *r*-stems), in each case at
least as well as the distinctive feminine types combined, since the
latter supplied only one apparent cognate. . . . When attention is
turned to the group of forms differing only through a single extension, one notes that the ratio of neuters to feminines among the
presumably earlier unextended forms is two and a half to one, the
same as that among the precise cognates, unless one include dupli-
cates, in which case it becomes greater. Again the apparently original neuters have all retained their gender unaltered in Hittite.
It is here that distinctive feminines become more numerous, for a
majority of those belonging to the first two groups occurred as $\bar{a}$-
stem extensions to forms neuter in Hittite. One therefore appears
entitled now to state that it is probable, though still less than
fully demonstrated, that Anatolian did not inherit a feminine."

Ivanov (1958: 611-612) argues that this archaic gender system
survives not only in Anatolian but also to a degree in Tocharian.
By the time of the oldest Tocharian documents, the earlier gender
system had been replaced by still another classificatory pattern involving a masculine, a feminine, and a common gender, "which is
identical with the masculine in the singular and with the feminine
in the plural" (1958: 611). Yet, Ivanov (1958: 611) concludes:
"Behind this later system we can clearly see the more ancient division of nouns into neuter gender, which has the same stem in the
nominative and in the oblique cases, and non-neuter (animate) gender,
in which these stems differ (a difference which is particularly
clear in Tocharian A)." As Szemerényi's remarks imply, other attested Indo-European languages provide somewhat more isolated pieces
of evidence which support the hypothesis that the gender classification system of Indo-European was originally binary. In addition to
the example which Szemerényi cites, Meillet (1931: 6) notes, for
instance, that although stems in *-o* are generally inherently non-
feminine, the existence of feminines in *-o* points to a time when
masculine-neuter stems were not differentiated from feminine ones:

Gk. *nuós*, Lat. *nurus*, Armen. *nu* 'daughter-in-law'; while the existence of masculines as members of the generally feminine *ā*- and *ī*-
stems leads to the same conclusion: Lat. *nauta* 'sailor', *agricola*
'farmer', *aurīga* 'charioteer', OCS *vojevoda* 'army commander', *sluga*
'manservant', Skt. *rathī́*-'charioteer'. Additional arguments in support of the late appearance of the feminine gender appear in Burrow
1973: 201-208.[2]

Since I shall need to refer to this fact later in a discussion of
the origin of the nominative singular suffix *-*s*, I should point out
that the tripartite division within the category of person in the
verb also appears to have developed gradually. Erhart (1970: 113)
therefore argues that in early Indo-European, "Es bestand wohl damals
noch kein Unterschied zwischen der 2. und der 3. Person, zwischen
dem Plural und dem Singular usw." After noting that "die Endungen
der 2. Person Sg. enthalten zum grösseren Teil ein *s*" (e.g. Skt. *-s*,
-si, Gk. *-s*, *-si*, Hitt. *-š*, *-ši*, Lat. *-s*, Go. *-s*, OCS *-ši*), that
*-*t* is also attested in the second person singular (e.g. Hitt. *-t*,
-ta, *-tari*, Toch. AB *-t*, A *-tār*, *-te*, B *-tar*, *-tai*, Skt. *-tha*, *-thās*,
Gk. *-thēs*, Go. *-t*) and the second person non-singular (dual-plural)
(e.g. Skt. *-ta*, *-tha*, *-tam*, Gk. *-te*, *-ton*, Hitt. *-teni*, Toch. A *-c*,
-cär, Lat. *-tis*, *-te*, Go. *-þ*, Lith. *-te*, *-ta*), that "in einigen Per-
sonalendungen der 2. Person (Sg. u. Pl.) stehen die Elemente *s* und
t(*h*) nebeneinander: gr. *stha*, het. *šta*, *šten*(*i*), toch. A *st*, B *sta*,
lat. *istī*, *istis*," and that *-*t* also occurs as a third person desinence (e.g. Skt. *-t*, *-ti*, Gk. *-ti*, Hitt. *-t*, *-zi*, Toch. A *-t*, Lat.
-t, Go. *-þ*, OCS *-tъ*, *-tъ*), he concludes: "Die Endungen der 2. Person
(aller drei Numeri) enthalten zum Teil denselben Kern. . . wie die
meisten Endungen der 3. Person Sing. Der Unterschied *t* (3. u. 2 Ps.)
: *th* (nur 2. Ps.) ist vielleicht in der Weise zu deuten, dass die
schon seit der pie. Periode bestehende phonetische Variation *t* ∿ *th*
später zur sekundären Differenzierung grammatischer Formen ausgenütz
worden ist" (1970: 56-58). It is important to note that *-*s* also
occurs dialectally in certain third person singular endings: e.g.
"Toch. A *pälkäṣ* (present tense), and Hitt. *pāiš* 'gave' and *dāiš*
'put' (preterit)" (Schmalstieg 1976b: 24). Krause and Thomas (1960:
259) etymologically connect other dialectal desinences with these:
"Eine ähnliche Übertragung findet man in an. *brýtr* (< urgerm.
*breutiz) 'du brichst' und 'er bricht', vielleicht auch in gr.
phérei (< idg. **bheresi*) sowie in altnorthumbr. *findes* (neben
findeþ)." Also to be included here are such Indo-Iranian forms as
Skt. *bhūyā́s* 'he should have been', *dhās* 'he put' and Old Persian *āiš*
'he went', *akunauš* 'he made' (Watkins 1962: 90-93). On the basis
of this evidence, Watkins (1962: 105) argues that "the classical
Indo-European 2 sg. ending -*s*(*i*) represents the old 3 sg. form,

ousted from 3 sg. to 2 sg. by the encroachment of a newer 3 sg. $-t(i)$. . . . The rigid paradigmatic structure for the three persons of the singular, $-m(i)$, $-s(i)$, $-t(i)$, belongs only to the latest period of Common Indo-European, and was completely achieved only after the separation of the dialects." What all of this seems to suggest to me is that the second-third (non-personal) category, whose original exponent was $*-\emptyset$, utilized $*-s$, and then both $*-s$ and $*-t$, as its desinences, with $*-s$ gradually becoming specialized primarily in the second person and $*-t$ in the third, although traces of the original vacillation between the suffixes are still seen in the dialects. That the original ending of the non-personal was $*-\emptyset$ is proposed by Watkins (1962:   90-106; 1969:   49-50). The occurrence of $*-\emptyset$ in the second person function is still attested in the singular imperative (*age 'lead':   Skt. *ája*, Gk. *áge*, Lat. *age*). Moreover, as Erhart (1970:   57-58) says: "In einem kleinen Teil der Fälle sind die Endungen der 3. Person Sg. akonsonantisch: aind. *a, e*, gr. *ei, e*, het. *i, a, ari*, toch. AB Ø, got. Ø, lit. *a* usw. . . . ; als ihre Bausteine sind der thematische Vokal und der Präsensdeterminativ *i* (bzw. *r*) zu erkennen."

2.2   Indo-European as an Ergative Language. At some time during its early stages, Indo-European seems to have passed through a period in which its structure was of the so-called ergative type. This proposal is nearly a century old, although after remaining outside conventional circles for many years, it seems now to be gaining more adherents, cf., e.g. Uhlenbeck 1901, Schuchardt 1905/06, Vaillant 1936, Knobloch 1954, Martinet 1962:   149-154, Savčenko 1967, Lyons 1971:   350-371, Marvan 1973a, 1973b, Shields 1978b, 1979c, Tchekhoff 1978, Schmidt 1979, Schmalstieg 1980:   166-188. In an ergative language, "The marked member of the transitive predication is the agent (marked by a special *active* or *ergative* case) and the unmarked member is the patient (marked by the 'nominative' or 'absolute' case, which also serves as the *substratum* of the intransitive predication)" (Aronson 1970:   291). The term *substratum* is defined as "the *one* 'substantial' participant required for the fulfillment of an action or process. . . . In essence it represents the neutralization of the opposition agent/patient" (Aronson 1970:   292). The ergative is considered a marked category since "it can function only as the grammatical subject of the sentence," while the absolute can function as both subject and object (Aronson 1970:   297).

As an ergative language, I believe that Indo-European possessed just two formally marked case categories: an absolute case in $*-N$ and an ergative case in $*-\emptyset$ and $*-r$. Now I realize that an ergative language with an ergative-case allomorph in $-\emptyset$ is somewhat unusual

since the unmarked case (absolute) would be expected to have no phonological realization. Indeed, Dixon (1979: 62) says: "If any
case in an 'ergative' language has zero realization, it will be absolutive." However, I find this statement to be far too strong.
Exceptions to the expected phonological manifestations of morphologically marked and unmarked forms are numerous. Matthews (1974:
152) thus notes: "Patterns of this kind are of particular interest
when they are repeated from one language to another. In the Nouns
of other Indo-European languages there is the same tendency for the
Plural and 'oblique' endings to be longer or more weighty than the
Singulars and Nominatives. Russian is merely one of the neatest
instances. There is also the non-cumulative pattern which we have
illustrated from Turkish (Ch. V), in which it is precisely the Singular and the Absolute—the latter functionally similar to a Nominative—which lack morphological identity altogether. It is this
general tendency which has tempted many scholars to accept the marking explanation. Again it is more usual, at least, for the 3rd
Singular to lack exponents in opposition to the 1st and 2nd than for
the 2nd, let us say, to lack them in opposition to the 3rd. But it
is a scholar's duty to be cautious and honest. Patterns of this
kind are sometimes confirmed, but often they are not. . . . In this
field it is very easy to 'explain' the things which fit, and relegate as exceptions or aberrations those which do not. Inflections
are basically arbitrary, just as roots and lexical formations are
also arbitrary. In the end one has to resign oneself to it." To be
sure, Dixon himself, after identifying the nominative as the unmarked
case in nominative-accusative languages, is forced to admit that
"there are a few well-attested instances where accusative is unmarked, while nominative involves a positive affix" (1979: 62).
Thus, in contrast to his strong assertion about the occurrence of
zero affixes in ergative languages, he merely states that "it is
nominative that most frequently has zero realization in an 'accusative' system" (1979: 62). The fact that there exist both nominative-accusative and ergative languages where both cases (nominative/
accusative, ergative/absolute) possess phonologically realized suffixes, cf. Dixon 1979: 72, also represents a violation of markedness patterns. Another argument against Dixon's proposed universal
lies in the relatively small number of ergative languages in existence. Comrie (1978: 392-393) laments that "by a combination of
geographical, social, and political accidents," the number of ergative languages is quite small and that the existing ones "have until
recently been largely neglected," resulting in a scarcity of information about ergative structure; while Dixon also admits that "languages with ergative case-marking" are "in a minority" (1979: 62)

and that "much more work is required on the description of ergative languages before all the suggestions . . . [made in Dixon 1979--K.S.] can be validated" (1979: 133). In demonstrating how important these facts are in our understanding of the nature of ergative lan- guages, Comrie (1978: 393) says: "One example will suffice to show how this scarcity of syntactic information can bias our general view of ergativity: the availability of a description of Dyirbal syntax, in the shape of Dixon's (1972) monograph, has revolutionized our view of ergativity, since for the first time it has become appar- ent that there is a language with near-consistent syntactic ergativ- ity. . . ." So, all in all, I do not feel that I am violating any linguistic universal when I suggest that *-∅ served as a marker of the ergative case in Indo-European. Even if such a state of affairs is not the most common one, one cannot at this time eliminate it as a possibility.

Moreoever, I believe that Indo-European was what Golab (1969: 6) calls a "reduced type" ergative language, like present-day Lesghian, in which "the . . . verb is not inflected either by persons or class indicators (affixes): it is neutral with respect to the nominal components of the sentence." Indeed, at this stage of development, the verb did not inflectionally express any of the traditional verb- associated categories of tense, aspect, mood, etc., although certain adverbial elements or particles, some of which could be used encli- tically and eventually became verbal suffixes, probably marked a number of these functions when they were not obviously inherent in the meaning of the verb itself, cf. Lehmann 1974: 177-186. If one ignores for the moment the ergative suffix *-r, it is obvious that a transitive sentence at this time would have had the following structure: NOUN-ERGATIVE (*-∅)—NOUN-ABSOLUTE (*-N)—VERB-TRANSI- TIVE, while an intransitive sentence would have had the form: NOUN- ABSOLUTE (*-N)—VERB-INTRANSITIVE.[3]

Many scholars have noted that the distributional distinction be- tween those nouns which can appear in the ergative case and the ab- solute case, and those nouns which can appear only in the absolute case is intimately connected with the semantic distinction between nouns referring to animate beings and nouns referring to inanimate objects, cf. Lyons 1971: 354-356. Simply, only the former may gen- erally appear in the ergative, or agentive, case for the obvious reason that animate beings alone can function pragmatically as agents. Although the Indo-Europeans had different views of the world around them from those of twentieth-century Westerners, I do not believe that these views are particularly important in tracing the development of the system of nominal classification, or gender, in Indo-European. That is, with some exceptions, I assume that the conceptual structure of the lexicon of a speaker of Indo-European was very much like that of contemporary man. For example, the entry for the lexical item *king* would contain the semantic markers (Male), (Animate), (Human), etc., while the entry for *stone* would contain (Physical Object), (Inanimate), etc. As far as the occurrence of lexical items in specific case-functions is concerned, in over-simplified transformational-generative terms, a word specified for animacy may appear under a node *N* (= Noun), which is, in turn, marked in some way for ergative-case function; and those nouns specified for inanimacy cannot generally appear under a nominal node marked for this case-function. Both animate and inanimate nouns are freely inserted under nominal nodes marked as representatives of the absolute case.

However, certain inherently inanimate nouns can act as agents; and, therefore, they can appear with regularity in the ergative case. Cruse (1973: 11) explains: "Comparing, for instance, *John overturned the dustbin* and *The wind overturned the dustbin*, it is difficult to see how *the wind* is any less of an agent than *John*: indeed, we commonly describe the sun, wind, frost, etc., as 'natural agents', without, surely, attributing animateness to them." Dixon (1979: 105-106) also refers to the existence of nouns of this type when he says: "Most languages have some transitive verbs whose major occurrence is with an animate agent, but which can also be used in an extended sense with an inanimate noun in the agent slot—e.g., *The wind closed the door*; *Sorrow is eating at my heart*. The central meanings of *close* and *eat* require animate agency; but the physical action of the wind can create the same impression as an animate agent, so that *the wind* is clearly regarded as an A NP [= 'the actual or potential "agent," who could (if anything could) initiate and control the activity' (Dixon 1979: 105)--K.S.] in *The wind closed the door*. And a language-particular metaphorical extension views the effects of sorrow as akin to 'eating' with respect to the institutionalized symbol 'heart'."

Thus, I believe that early Indo-European possessed three primary semantic classes of nouns whose meanings were relevant in defining the case-functions that each of these nouns could assume: animate, inanimate, and inanimate agent (or natural agent). Only the inanimate nouns were generally excluded from appearing in the ergative case.

I should point out that in his discussion of agency, Cruse (1973: 16) observes that "indisputably inanimate nouns" may function as agents when certain verbs are used, e.g., *The bullet smashed John's collarbone*. Therefore, "It seems. . . that inanimate objects can, as it were, acquire a temporary 'agentivity' by virtue of their

kinetic (or other) energy." In similar sentences in ergative languages, such nouns may also assume the ergative function. However,
"In general, the causation of some external effect seems to be necessary for this type of 'agentivity' to be detectable"; and thus nouns
of this type are not really true agents, i.e. objects which perform
actions "using their own energy in carrying out the action" (Cruse
1973: 21). Their use as agents (and hence as ergative-case forms)
is exceptional, being limited to co-occurrence with a relatively
small number of transitive verbs whose semantic structure is responsible for the external causation just noted.

2.3   From Ergative to Nominative-Accusative. The ergative system
of early Indo-European gradually developed into the nominative-
accusative system which is attested in the dialects. The change
crucially involved the generalization of the ergative marker *-$\emptyset$ as
the habitual indicator of the subject in the animate and the natural
agent nominal classes. That is, the typical ergative structure with
a transitive verb, NOUN-ERGATIVE (*-$\emptyset$)—NOUN-ABSOLUTE (*-N)—VERB
TRANSITIVE, exerted a strong analogical influence on the typically
intransitive construction, NOUN-ABSOLUTE (*-N)—VERB-INTRANSITIVE,
yielding, NOUN-ABSOLUTE (*-$\emptyset$)—VERB INTRANSITIVE. Obviously, the
extension affected only those nouns that could generally appear in
the ergative case. I would like to suggest that the interpretation
of *-$\emptyset$ as the marker of the subject in the customary Indo-European
sense (and thus as the desinence of the nominative case) was primarily motivated by the fact that the *-$\emptyset$ of the ergative case was
identified with the *-$\emptyset$ non-personal suffix of the verb, which
emerged after the introduction of the personal (first person) verbal
marker *-N (cf., e.g. sg. Skt. -m, -mi, Gk. -n, -mi, OCS -v (< *-on),
-mv, Lat. -m; pl. Skt. -$masi$, -mas, -$m\breve{a}$, Gk. -mes, Lat. -mus, Lith.
-ma), whose origin may have been pronominal, cf. Schmalstieg 1976b:
23. Since, as I shall argue below, the original concordial system
of Indo-European was largely based on assonance, the recognition of
a non-personal verbal suffix *-$\emptyset$ which was not only "homophonous"
with the original ergative suffix *-$\emptyset$ but also by chance occurred
with it in a relationship typically constrained by concordial government naturally led to this general replacement of *-N by *-$\emptyset$.
The inanimate nouns, which never or only rarely appeared in the
ergative case and thus with the suffix *-$\emptyset$, continued to preserve
*-N as the marker of the subject in intransitive constructions.
That the distribution of certain case-forms does indeed affect the
diachronic development of a language in ways similar to this is historically attested. "Thus it has been remarked by Behaghel, Bojunga,
and Tegnér that in the G. n-declension the old nom. without -n has

held its own in names of living beings only: *bote, erbe, knabe,*
while inanimates have generalized the oblique cases [in the nominative and the oblique functions--K.S.]: *bogen, magen, tropfen"* because of the relative rarity of nominative inanimates (Jespersen
1935: 239). Likewise, "The dative is more often used in words denoting living beings than with inanimates; hence the acc. forms
found in the oldest English, *mec, þec, usic, eowic* were early ousted
by the dat. *me, þe, us, eow* (now *me, thee, us, you*), and somewhat
later the old datives *hire (her), him, hem* (mod. *'em), hwam (whom)*
displace the old accusatives *heo, hine, hie, hwane. . . .* On the
other hand, in the neuter it is the old accusatives *hit (it), that,
what* that are preserved at the cost of the datives" (Jespersen 1935:
239).

Because of their identity of function as markers of the subject
of intransitive verbs, *-∅ and *-*N* were interpreted as the indicators of the same case, when this construction was employed. In what
I shall now describe as objective function, instead of accusative
function, for reasons that will become clear shortly, all nouns continued to utilize the suffix *-*N*. However, the occurrence of *-∅
and *-*N* in the same functional environment also led to their interpretation as exponents of some kind of explicit opposition: NOUN-
NOMINATIVE (*-∅)—VERB-INTRANSITIVE versus NOUN-NOMINATIVE (*-*N*)—
VERB-INTRANSITIVE. Although a connection between animacy and the
*-∅ suffix of the ergative (> nominative) case as well as a connec-
tion between inanimacy and the inability of nouns to appear with
this inflectional formant was probably always sensed, to some degree,
by speakers of Indo-European, this sharply distinctive contrast in
the use of the terminations *-∅ and *-*N* resulted in the direct association of animacy with the nominative marker *-∅ and of inanimacy
with the nominative marker *-*N*, since most nouns with a nominative
in *-∅ shared the semantic property of animacy, while those forming
a nominative in *-*N* shared the property of inanimacy. Thereafter,
*-∅ and *-*N* were "portmanteau morphs," "which belong simultaneously
to two (or, theoretically, more) morphemes, and have simultaneously
the meaning of both" (Hockett 1957: 236). That is, these suffixes
now indicated not only case but also gender.

The three semantic classes of early Indo-European were at this
juncture formally marked according to the following schema:

	animate	inanimate	inanimate (natural) agent
nominative	*-∅	*-*N*	*-∅
objective	*-*N*	*-*N*	*-*N*

Obviously, the inanimate agent class represented an incongruity in
the newly emerging gender system since nouns of this type were in-

animate but nevertheless formed a nominative in *-∅. This inconsistency was rectified through the operation of analogy. The identity of forms of the nominative and the objective which was exemplified in the inanimate class was generalized to the inanimate agent nouns, but the autonomy of the latter group was preserved by generalizing *-∅ as an objective marker. Most probably, the common use of the natural agent nouns, like the animates, as subjects of transitive verbs contributed to their retention of the characteristic animate ending *-∅. Thus, it seems that the opposition *animate* : *inanimate* came to be realized paradigmatically rather than directly through individual inflectional formants.

The natural agent nominal class retains many of its earlier characteristics in the historical dialects. The inflectional pattern of the class as well as its semantic properties of inanimacy and inherent agentivity (evidenced in its members' seeming capacity for unprovoked action) can still be observed: e.g. Skt. *ákṣi* 'eye'; Skt. *kravís*, Gk. *kréas* 'flesh'; Skt. *mánas*, Gk. *ménos* 'mind'; Skt. *ápas*, Lat. *opus* 'work'; Skt. *jắnu*, Gk. *gónu*, Lat. *genu* 'knee'; Skt. *śrávas*, Gk. *kléos*, OCS *slovo* 'word, report'; Skt. *nắma*, Lat. *nōmen*, Hitt. *laman* 'name'; Skt. *ắs*, Lat. *ōs* 'mouth'; Skt. *bhắs* 'light', Lat. *fās* 'divine law'(cf. Brugmann 1911: 149); Skt. *hṛd-*, Lat. *cor*, Gk. *kễr* 'heart'; Gk. *pûr*, Umbr. *pir*, Armen. *hur* 'fire'; Gk. *húdōr*, Umbr. *utur*, Hitt. *watar* 'water'; Skt. *ásṛk*, Gk. *éar*, Lat. *asser* 'blood'; etc. However, a fairly large group of inanimate nouns with an identical formal structure are clearly not agents in any sense: e.g. Skt. *mádhu* 'honey', Gk. *méthu* 'intoxicating drink'; Gk. *gála* (< *gálakt*), Lat. *lac* (< *lact*) 'milk'; OLat. *sale*, Go. *salt* 'salt'; Skt. *śákṛt*, Gk. *kópros* (> masc.) 'dung'; Skt. *áyas*, Lat. *aes*, Go. *aiz* 'metal'; etc. I would suggest that these are later analogical formations. Because many of the natural agent nouns themselves denote material, mass, or substance, semantically similar inanimate nouns like these with originally different formal structures were remodeled on analogy with them, gradually reducing the close relationship between the formal structure of this nominal group and the notion "agent." Still other nouns of this type owe their dialectal class memberships to further analogical changes. Thus, throughout the period of Indo-European unity and beyond, the inanimate agent class, defined formally if not semantically, continued to stand in contrast to an inanimate class which formed its nominative-objective in *-N (cf. Hitt. *yukan*, Lat. *jugum*, Gk. *dzugón* 'yoke'), although the membership of the second group was substantially reduced during the course of time; for in the historical period only the *o*-stem inanimate nouns continue to retain any trace of the archaic nominative-objective suffix *-N. Perhaps the relative

rarity of inanimate nouns with the suffix *-N in other stem classes,
in comparison to those showing the ending *-∅, led to their eventual
elimination there, just as the preponderance of inanimate nouns with
a nominative-objective in *-∅ in the o-stems may have eventually led
to the generalization of this suffix throughout this declensional
class. Substantial analogical remodeling of the inanimate nouns was
to be expected after the clear distinction between natural agent
nouns and true inanimate nouns had come to be blurred, due at first
to rather minor analogical changes like the one involving the inclusion of mass nouns in general in the natural agent category. Other
processes which can alter the gender class memberships of nouns are
discussed in Shields 1979a.

 Baltic, Slavic, and Hittite appear to show neuter o-stem forms
with *-∅ as a nominative-objective (> accusative) singular suffix:
Lith. gĕra 'good', OP wissa 'all', OCS mešto 'place', Russ. xorošo
'good', Hitt. marsa 'bad', tannatta 'empty'. Only the Slavic group
yields firm evidence for the *-∅ desinence in the neuter nouns, since
the occurrence of this ending in these other Indo-European subfami-
lies is limited to adjectives. I would explain these constructions
as resulting from a specifically dialectal analogical extension of
-∅ to the o-stems, motivated by its appearance in this function in
all other stem classes of neuter nouns. The rather imperfect nature
of the extension is demonstrated especially by co-existing forms in
-N in both Baltic and Hittite: OP wissan 'all', Hitt. tannattan
'empty'. Other hypotheses have also been offered in explanation of
this secondary dialectal development, cf., e.g. Endzelīns 1971: 167-
168, Kronasser 1956: 107-108, Neu 1969: 240-241, and Schmalstieg
1976a: 71-72.

 It should be noted, before considering the development of the ergative suffix *-r, that the Hittite data presented in Tchekhoff 1978
indirectly imply that Indo-European possessed a special class of
natural agent nouns, although Tchekhoff interprets the significance
of these data somewhat differently. In Hittite, inanimate nouns cannot serve as subjects of transitive verbs; they can serve only as
subjects of intransitive verbs or as objects of transitive verbs.
However, certain conceptually inanimate nouns, "par exemple, les
éléments naturels, eau, feu, etc. les parties du corps, les bâtiments,
et les notions correspondant à des abstractions de toutes sortes,"
i.e. those which "seront conçues comme capables d'activité" (1978:
228), or the natural agents, can serve as subjects of transitive
verbs by means of two processes: (1) a special lexical form of the
word, formally marked as animate, appears when the word is used as a
subject of a transitive verb, whereas another lexical form, marked
as inanimate, is used elsewhere, cf. "'l'eau', animé habas, inanimé

wadar" (1978: 229), and (2) the derivational suffix *-ant* is used to
form animate nouns from generally inanimate stems, cf. "*udne* 'pays,
inanimé' ∿ *udne-ent-* 'pays, animé'. Ce suffixe se construit sur
les cas obliques à nasale des hétéroclites en *-r/n-*" (1978: 229).
I would argue that Hittite has simplified the Indo-European syntactic
rule that only conceptually animate and natural agent nouns, and not
conceptually inanimate nouns even if they were formally identical to
the natural agents, could regularly appear as subjects of transitive
verbs by permitting *formally* animate nouns alone in this function
and thereby eliminating the frequent occurrence of one subset of the
inanimate class (the natural agents) as well as the infrequent occurrence of the other subset (the true inanimates) in this environment.
However, the semantic necessity of allowing natural agent nouns to
appear as subjects of transitive verbs resulted in their partial
formal assimilation into the animate class. In other words, a sim-
plification in one component of the grammar (syntax) led to a com-
plication in another (morphology), cf. King 1969: 86-87. Thus,
despite the innovative character of the processes involved, Hittite
shows the tendency for natural agent nouns to differentiate themselves formally from the true inanimates and the animates.

2.3   The Ergative Suffix *-r*. My hypothesis that early Indo-European possessed an ergative suffix *-r* is largely predicated on the
existence of the so-called *-r-/-n-*-stem nouns. The archaic nature of
this type of neuter noun is acknowledged by Benveniste (1935: 3),
who refers to this declensional class as "le vestige le plus archaï-
que de l'ancienne flexion indo-européenne." In this class of nouns,
as it is attested, the nominative-accusative is formed by a stem in
-r while the oblique cases show a stem in *-n*. "This ancient type
of neuter noun is tending to obsolescence in the earliest Sanskrit,
as it is in Greek and most of the other languages. In Hittite on
the other hand, which presents here, as so often, a more archaic
stage of Indo-European, the system is unimpaired. The system as
found in Hittite contains simple *r/n* stems with this alternation,
e.g. *ešḫar* 'blood', gen. sg. *ešnaš*, also a series of compound suffixes formed by the addition of these suffixes to stems in *u*, *m*, *s*,
t, namely *-war*, *-mar*, *-sar*, *-tar*. . . . This early system of neuter
nouns exists only in fragments in other IE languages, but an abun-
dance of suffixes containing *r* and *n* have these primitive neuter
types as their ultimate source" (Burrow 1973: 127).[4] It would
seem that a large number of nouns of this type represent what I have
termed the "inanimate agents," as the following attested lexical
items (some of which I have already cited in their nominative-accusative form as examples of inanimate agent nouns) indicate: Hitt.

watar, gen. *wetenas̆*, Gk. *hûdōr*, gen. *-atos* (< *-n̥tos*), Skt. *udan-*,
gen. *udn-âs*, Umbr. *utur*, Alb. *une* (< *udne*) 'water'; Hitt. *es̆ḫar*,
gen. *es̆nas̆*, Skt. *ásr̥-k*, gen. *asn-âs*, OLat. *asser*, Latvian *asins*
'blood'; Skt. *yâkr̥-t*, gen. *yakn-âs*, "Lat. *iecur*, gen. **iecinis* beside *iecoris* (whence the blend *iecinoris*)" (Wakelin 1974: 109)
'liver'; Skt. *ûdhar*, gen. *ûdhn-as*, Gk. *hoûthar*, gen. *-atos* (< *-n̥tos*),
Lat. *ūber*, gen. *-eris* for *-inis* 'udder'; Gk. *éar*, *eîar*, gen. *éaros*
(< *wĕsr̥*), Lith. *vasarà* ('summertime'), Lat. *uēr* (< *wēsr̥*), Skt.
vasan-tâ-, OCS *vesna* 'springtime'; Gk. *mārē*, Lat. *manus*, Umbr. acc.
pl. *manf*, ON *mund* 'hand'; "Lat. *femur*, gen. *feminis* (beside *femoris*
with generalized *r*) 'thigh'" (Wakelin 1974: 109); Gk. *phréār*, gen.
-atos (< *phre[f]ar-atos*), Armen. *ałbiur* (< *bhrēur̥*), Go. *brunna*
'fountain, source'; Hitt. *paḫḫur*, gen. *paḫḫuenas̆*, Umbr. *pir*, OIr.
ūr, Gk. *pûr*, Go. *fōn*, gen. *funins* 'fire'; Skt. *áhar*, gen. *áhn-as*,
Avest. gen. *asn-q̥m* 'day'.[5]

The general analysis of the development of Indo-European nominal
inflection which I have already presented provides a natural explanation of the existence of nouns of this type and their apparent membership in the inanimate agent class, if it is assumed that early
Indo-European possessed an ergative suffix *-r*. Simply, there would
have existed in early Indo-European nouns which could accept terminations in *-r* (ergative) and *-N* (absolute), in addition to those
which could accept *-∅* (ergative) and *-N* (absolute), and those
which could accept only *-N* (absolute). When the nominative-accusative system arose because of the interpretation of *-∅* as a non-
personal verbal suffix in concord with the nominal suffix *-∅*, the
now nominative ending *-r* would have had some difficulty becoming
integrated into the new inflectional system. In order to remedy
this situation, a reanalysis of forms containing this suffix occurred: NOUN + *r* > NOUN - *r* + ∅ (where + = a morphological boundary).[6]
That is, *-r* lost its inflectional value and became a stem-forming
element. In the animate class this led to the formation (or perhaps
augmentation) of *r*-stem nouns with a new *-∅* ending in the nominative and the old *-N* suffix in the objective. An example of an animate noun "with the simple *r*-suffix is seen in [Skt.--K.S.] *nâr-*
'man, warrior' (Gk. *anḗr*, Umbrian *ner-*, etc.)" (Burrow 1973: 141).
But in the natural agent class, where *-∅* was also being extended to
the objective function as well, speakers used the same process where-
by the old nominative marker *-r* was better integrated into the
nominal system as a model for the extension of *-∅* to mark the objective function in those nouns which originally possessed a nominative in *-r*: NOUN + *N* > NOUN -*N* + ∅. This led naturally to the
formation of a type of noun which alternated its stem-element
(-*r*- ∿ -*N*-) according to the case-function assumed by the noun.

After the number of case categories began to increase in Indo-European, the alternate stem in *-N- became limited to the oblique cases,
whose functions, along with that of the accusative, were originally
indicated by the objective marker *-N. Since, in later stages of
the language, inanimate nouns shared a common form for the nominative and the accusative, they exerted analogical pressure on the
original natural agent nouns to conform to this pattern, thereby
bringing about the specialization of the ancient objective stem in
*-N- to the oblique function.

It should be emphasized that the addition of an inflectional suffix (in this situation *-∅) to another inflectional suffix, with the
reinterpretation of the latter as a stem-formant, is perhaps attested
in the historical dialects: "In Hittite we encounter forms like
me-mi-ya-na-aš, in which the 'final ending' is not added to the stem,
but rather to a stem plus ending; *me-mi-ya-na-aš*, though morphologically the genitive of *me-mi-ya-aš*, consists of a genitive formed
from an apparent accusative *me-mi-ya-an*" (Lehmann 1958: 200).

Perhaps the addition of *-∅ to the inflected form in *-N in the
natural agent class explains the appearance of *-N- as a stem-element
of the oblique cases in other stem-classes of neuter nouns, resulting
in the creation of other heteroclitic declensions. In this regard
Burrow (1973: 227) says: "In the case of *vā́ri* 'water' the *n*-suffix
is added to instead of being substituted for the *i*-suffix (gen. sg.
vā́riṇas). This process appears commonly in neuter *u*-stems: *dā́ru*
drúṇas, *mádhu* 'honey', *mádhunas*, etc., and its antiquity is guaran-
teed by similar formations elsewhere: Gk. *dóru*, *dóratos* (*dorwṇtos*,
with the additional *t*-suffix characteristic of Greek)." In other
words, a form terminated in *-i-∅ in the nominative and *-i-N in the
objective at times came to be reinterpreted as having *-in-∅ in the
latter case just as nouns which originally showed *-r in the nominative case developed an objective in *-N-∅ through reanalysis. Analogical formations of this type thus came to stand beside those
characteristic of natural agent nouns with an original nominative in
*-∅, e.g. Skt. gen. *mádhvas*, resulting from the simple replacement
of *-N by *-∅ in the objective. Forms like Skt. *ásthi* 'bone', which
"substitute an *n*-stem outside the nom. acc. sg.: *ásthi* : *asthnás*
'bone', etc." (Burrow 1973: 227), have probably undergone the same
analogical development but show a complete replacement of the *-i-
stem-element by *-N- on analogy with the *r-/n*-stems. That nouns of
these other heteroclitic declensions have an origin in the natural
agent class is suggested, e.g., by the following attested forms:
Ved. *hā́rdi*, Hitt. *karti-*, Armen. *sirt* (< *kḗrdi-), Gk. *kardía*, Go.
hairtō, gen. *hairtins* (< *kḗrd-en-) 'heart'; Avest. *uši-* (in *uši-
bya*), Lith. *ausìs*, Lat. *auri-*, Gk. gen. *oúatos*, pl. *oúata* (< *ous-

n̥-t-), Go. ausō, Armen. unkn 'ear'; Lat. axis, Lith. ašìs, OP assis, OCS osъ (< *aks-i-), OHG ahsa, Gk. áksōn (< *aks-en-) 'axle'; Skt. ákṣi, gen. akṣnás 'eye'.

There are some other data which independently suggest that the suffix *-r possessed an original ergative, or agentive, value. For example, in regard to the suffixes traditionally reconstructed as *-er and *-ter which appeared in animate nouns, e.g. *pəter- 'father': Skt. pitár-, Armen. hair, Lat. pater, Go. fadar, Gk. patḗr; *daiu̯er- 'brother-in-law': Skt. dēvár-, Gk. dā́ēr, Brugmann (1891: 377) says: "The nouns in which these suffixes occur are, with comparatively few exceptions, nomina agentis or names of kindred. The former class has -ter- throughout." However, Brugmann (1904: 330) emphasizes that their use in kinship terms is secondary: "Ihr uridg. Formans -(t)er-, -(t)or-, -(t)r̥-, -(t)r̥- hatte ursprünglich mit dem Verwandtschaftsbegriff an sich nichts zu thun. Zufälliger Gebrauch in dem einen oder andern der Wörter für Vater, Mutter usw. liess es mit der Funktion, Verwandtschaftsnamen zu bilden, schöpferisch werden"; this use stems from their primary function of deriving nomina agentis. Now I believe that the suffix which is seen here is the agentive, or ergative, *-r in contamination with the linking vowel *-o/e- (*-or-) or the union consonant *-t-, cf. Kurylowicz 1964: 195, (*-tr̥-). The stage of development of the Indo-European language at which these suffixes originated predates the emergence of ablaut variation as a morphological device (a matter I shall consider below), and so certain alternate forms of these affixes appeared at a later date. Apparently the origin of these suffixes lies in a reanalysis of the stem-element *-r- (< ergative *-r) as a derivational suffix with agentive meaning. Because many of the nouns to which *-r- was affixed possessed a natural agentive denotation, as their ability to appear in the ergative would suggest, this formal characteristic of these nouns was interpreted as the exponent of this semantic characteristic.

Moreover, there were in Indo-European nomina instrumenti in *-tro- (union consonant + *-r- suffix + thematic vowel): "skr. mán-tra-ḥ, av. mą-θrō 'formule religieuse, prière', ... gr. áro-tro-n, irl. arathar, arm. arawr (de *arā-tro-), lat. arā-tru-m, . . . " (Meillet 1964: 273), and *-dhro- ("aus dem 'Determinativ' -dh- + -ro-" [Brugmann 1904: 334]): Gk. báthron 'base', árthron 'joint', Lat. crībrum 'sieve'. Now Brugmann (1891: 461) emphasizes that there exists an intimate connection between nomina agentis and nomina instrumenti: "Nomina agentis are often used to denote an instrument, this being regarded as if it were a living performer of the action: cp. Mod.H.G. träger used both for the person who carries and the means of carrying (beams and the like)." I would like

to propose that these suffixes, too, have their origin as markers
of *nomina agentis*, only later becoming specialized as indicators of
nomina instrumenti. The natural agent class of nouns would especially show this same ambiguity (agent and instrument), and perhaps
it was here that such a development had its start. This might explain why these suffixes appear "gewöhnlich als Neutr." (Brugmann
1904: 334), although their occurrence "with some masc. and fem."
(Buck 1933: 326) belies their early appearance with nouns of the
animate class also, as would be expected if they originally served
to mark *nomina agentis* and if they ultimately derive from the ergative suffix *-r.[7]

Finally, it has long been suggested that the verbal affixes in
*-r have a nominal origin: "Damit treten die r-Formen [of the verb
--K.S.] in den grossen Zusammenhang der Nomina auf -*er*, -*u̯er*, -*ser*,
-*ter* mit ihren verschiedenen Vokalabstufungen, die zu den ältesten
Erscheinungen der idg. Morphologie gehören" (Hartmann 1954: 200).
To be sure, the antiquity of these verbal forms seems hard to deny,
as Wyatt (1972: 693) points out in his review of Watkins 1969: "It
appears that Watkins believes that r-forms are later or dialectal.
But this seems difficult, for a dialectal entity embracing Hittite/
Latin/Celtic/Tocharian would seem unusual, and if true, indicative
of archaism rather than innovation." I also subscribe to the position that the verbal ending *-r is archaic and bears an etymological
relationship to nominal suffixes in *-r, although I see the nature
of this relationship in very different terms from traditional ac-
counts. It is often argued, cf., e.g. Brugmann 1916: 665, Meillet
1964: 235, Schmalstieg 1976b: 30, that verbal forms in *-r were
originally impersonals.[8] Of course, an impersonal verb is one "denoting action by an unspecified or indefinite agent, normally used
only in the third singular" (Pei 1966: 121). I would suggest that
the agentive signification inherent in such Indo-European impersonal
verbal forms in *-r derives from the original agentive value of the
nominal suffix *-r. Simply, because linguistic change is a slow and
variable process, i.e., "it begins as a rule that sometimes operates
and sometimes does not" (Bailey 1973: 157), it would not be unexpected, then, that the interpretation of *-$\emptyset$ as a non-personal
verbal desinence in concord with a nominal suffix *-$\emptyset$, the generalization of *-$\emptyset$ as a nominative marker in the animate and the natural
agent classes of nouns, and the loss of *-r as a nominative marker
would occur gradually. Since these changes were not immediately
effected, the continued existence of *-r as a nominative suffix and
the establishment of an assonance concord relationship between the
animate and the natural agent nominative case in *-$\emptyset$ and the non-
personal verb in *-$\emptyset$ may have led at times to the analogical exten-

sion of *-*r* to the verb as a desinence, despite the trend to gener-
alize the *-∅ form because the non-personal verb itself naturally
and generally possessed a *-∅ ending. Thus, two possible subject-
verb constructions containing animate or natural agent nouns would
have occurred, although the first was probably rather infrequent:

NOUN + *r* _____VERB + *r*
NOUN + ∅ _____VERB + ∅.

The initial one completely disappeared when the nominative in *-*r*
was lost. Of course, the following constructions were impossible
ones since they violated the constraint of assonance concord between
subject and verb:

*NOUN + *r*_____VERB + ∅
*NOUN + ∅_____VERB + *r*.

But because the inanimate class of nouns never did participate in
this type of concordial government, constructions of both the following types would have been present in the language, although inanimate
nouns did not appear as subjects of transitive verbs with any regularity:

NOUN + *N* _____VERB + ∅
NOUN + *N* _____VERB + *r*.

The first construction here, obviously the more common, came to be
the fundamental means by which the subject-verb relation was expressed when nouns of the inanimate class were involved. However,
the rather infrequent second construction, with a secondary analogical origin, apparently underwent reanalysis and subsequent morphological specialization, resulting in its retention in the language.
That is, the *-*N* of the noun came to be viewed as an objective
marker, which was identical in form with the nominative in the inanimate class, thereby yielding a true impersonal verbal form, cf.
"*discipulum laudatur* 'one praises the pupil'" (Kurylowicz 1964: 73).
Probably the general rarity of inanimate nouns as subjects of transitive verbs gave impetus to this reanalysis.

NOTES

[1]The ambiguity of the Hittite orthographic system, however, tends
to detract from the substantiating value of these Hittite forms.
Since vocalic length is not consistently indicated (if it is indicated at all), cf. Sturtevant 1933: 63 and Kronasser 1956: 43, these
Hittite words in plural function might be cognate with plural forms
like Avest. *vacā* 'words', *nāmąn* 'names', which show etymological
vocalic length as a marker of plurality, cf. Burrow 1973: 237.
[2]Throughout this monograph I shall assume that gender itself is
realized formally through the occurrence (or absence) of certain
overt markers which indicate the class memberships of the nominal

forms to which they are related in a sentence.   In the Indo-European
languages these markers typically involve: (1) derivational or inflectional suffixes added to nominal stems, (2) modes of adjectival
concord, and (3) modes of pronominal reference. Since the first of
these indicators is frequently sporadic and inconsistent in the
dialects, there is a general acceptance of the fact that at the cen-
ter of Indo-European nominal gender, at least in later stages of the
language, is adjectival and pronominal agreement.

[3]This example is not intended to make any claims about the word
order of the Indo-European sentence at this evolutionary stage. The
choice of word order, therefore, has no significance, although Lehmann (1973: 183-184) does argue that Indo-European was verb-final in
its early period of development.

[4]However, as Schindler (1975: 211) notes: "The *r/n*-stems fall
into two different categories: a) Stems in a simple suffix *-er/n*
preceded directly by the root (*$ed-er/n-* 'water' etc.). b) Stems
in a complex suffix of the form *-Cer/n*: *-uer/n, -mer/n, -ter/n,
-ser/n*. It is often impossible to attribute a given form to one or
the other of these categories."

[5]See Benveniste 1935: 3-22 for a catalogue of Indo-European *r-/n*-
stem nouns. Many others listed there are natural agents; but because their etymologies are less certain than those which appear
here, I have omitted them in this presentation, e.g., "véd. *kápr̥t* n.
'pénis' se range dans le même groupe que *śákr̥t yákr̥t*, quoique la
forme à *-n-* ne soit pas connue" (Benveniste 1935: 9).

[6]Of course, according to Mańczak (1958: 321), there exists an analogical tendency such that "les désinences zéro sont plus souvent
remplacées par les désinences pleines que vice versa." However, it
should be emphasized that even Manczak (1958: 322-323) admits that
in those historical grammars whose data served as the basis of his
hypothesis, there are frequently (as high as 28 percent of all cases
of analogical change involving *-∅*) attested instances of *-∅* being
extended to forms originally possessing phonologically-realized endings.   The fact that the Indo-European nominal system was in a state
of transition at this time may have additionally contributed to this
development.

[7]There also exist parallel *nomina agentis* and *nomina instrumenti*
suffixes in *-l-*: *-lo- (nomina agentis)*: ". . . lat. *bib-ulus,
créd-ulus, trem-ulus*, d'où les participes slaves et arméniens en
-lo-, tels que v. sl. *neslŭ (jesmĭ)* 'j'ai porté' et arm. *gereal
(em)* 'j'ai pris' et l'infinitif arménien, *gerel* 'prendre'" (Meillet
1964: 267); *-tlo- (nomina instrumenti)*: Lith. *árkla-s* (> masc.)
'plow', "Ahd. *wadal* 'Wedel' urgerm. *$aplo-* (W. *u̯e-* 'wehen'). Im
Ital. (und Lit.) wurde *-tlo-* zu *-klo-*, woraus *-kr̂o-* hinter *l*, z.B.
lat. *lavācrum*" (Brugmann 1904: 334); *-dhlo- (nomina instrumenti)*:
"lat. *stabulum* ahd. *stal* 'Stall', . . . lat. . . . *caelum = *caidlom
. . . *exōrābulum, suscitābulum*; Čech. *šidlo* aksl. *šilo* 'Pfrieme' zu
lat. *sūbula (suere)*, poln. *czerpadło* aksl. *črъpalo* 'Schöpfgefäss'"
(Brugmann 1904: 334). I believe that the *-l-* of these suffixes
may be related to the agentive suffix *-r-*. As Buck (1933: 38)
notes, liquids are especially subject to dissimilation, cf. "L.
peregrīnus > late *pelegrīnus* (cf. NE *pilgrim*)." Thus, variant dis-
similated suffixes in *-l-* may have become autonomous elements in
the language. "IE *r* and *l* are partially merged in Sanskrit" (Buck
1933: 131), while "in Iranian IE *r* and *l* appear indiscriminately
as *r*" (Burrow 1973: 83); but these developments seem to be specifically Indo-Iranian.

[8]This hypothesis regarding the origin of the *r*-forms of the verb
in impersonal constructions has been seriously questioned, cf., e.g.
Flobert 1975: 464-467; but as Flobert (1975: 466) himself notes:
"L'impersonnel qui a encore bénéficié de la caution de Brugmann, de
Meillet et de la plupart des comparatistes, poursuit aujourd'hui sa

carrière." It should be emphasized, however, that even if this theory is untenable, the validity of my proposal concerning the appearance of neuter r-/n-stem nouns in unaffected. I am merely demonstrating in this paragraph that my analysis can be extended to include an explanation of these problematical verbal forms as well.

3 The Enrichment of the Case System

3.   So far, I have outlined the development of Indo-European from
an ergative language to a nominative-accusative one with a nominative case[1] in *-∅ and *-N, and an objective case in *-N. The language at this time possessed no inflections which indicated number
distinctions; and its nouns were classified into only two gender
categories—animate and inanimate (the distinction between natural
agents and true inanimates having become blurred). Even at this
early date, one can probably assume that speakers of the language
had begun to group nouns also by the final sound of the stem. Thus,
in all of the reconstructions which follow, I shall acknowledge
three major nominal declensions on the basis of their inflection in
later stages of Indo-European and the dialects: (1) consonant stems,
(2) vocalic resonant stems, and (3) vowel stems. In this latter
group I place stems in *-o (*-e) and in *-ă. That Indo-European had
nominal forms in *-ă is suggested by substantives like Gk. númpha
'nymph', nephēlegerêta 'cloud-gatherer', hippēláta 'horseman', peîra
'test', géphūra 'bridge', Umbr. Tursa 'Tursa', Lat. mensa 'table'
(also perhaps resulting from the iambic law), OCS ženo 'woman', glavo
'head', etc. These nouns function as nominatives and vocatives in
Greek and Italic, while Old Church Slavic utilizes them only as vocatives.   At a later date the ă-declension was generally assimilated
into the relatively recent ā-stems.

The nominative in *-∅ is still attested in the consonant stem nominative singular masculine and feminine (Gk. kúōn 'dog', Go. guma
'man', Lat. māter 'mother', Skt. dâtā 'giver') and in the nominative-
accusative singular neuter (Gk. méthu 'intoxicating drink', Skt.
mádhu 'honey', Go. faihu 'cattle, money'), while the nominative suffix *-N is seen in the nominative-accusative singular neuter of the
o-stems (Gk. dzugón, Skt. yugám, Lat. jugum 'yoke'). The objective
ending *-N is attested in the neuter forms just noted and in the
accusative singular masculine and feminine (Skt. vŕkam, Gk. lúkon,
Lat. lupum, Lith. vilką 'wolf'). As an original objective desinence,

this nasal suffix marked, in addition to the direct object (accusative), those functions which were later assumed by the genitive, ablative, dative, instrumental, and locative cases. The dialects yield a great deal of evidence in support of this conclusion.

3.1 *-N* as a Marker of the Genitive-Ablative. In the Indo-European languages a special form for the ablative case is generally found only in the singular of the *o*-stem declension, with the same desinence as that of the genitive singular serving in the ablative singular elsewhere. The *o*-stem ablative ending is traditionally reconstructed as *-ē/ōd* (Skt. *vŕ̥kād*, Lat. *lupō*, Lith. *vilko* 'wolf',[2] OLat. *Gnaivōd* 'Gnaivus', Gk. [adv.] *hôpō*, Go. [adv.] *hvaþrō* 'whence'), cf. Brugmann 1904: 383-383; and the non-thematic suffix of the genitive-ablative is reconstructed as *-(e/o)s* (Skt. *nāvás* 'ship', Lat. *hominis* 'man', Lith. *akmeñs* 'stone'). I shall consider the origin of this sigmatic suffix shortly. Now if the genitive and the ablative originally constituted a single morphologically realized category, as implied by the dual function of the ending *-(e/o)s*, then one might expect the same two functions to be expressed by the traditionally reconstructed genitive (> genitive plural) suffix *-ŏ̄N* (a contamination of the thematic vowel plus *-N*, cf. Schmalstieg 1977b: 130). I believe that there exists substantive evidence that this was indeed the actual situation in Indo-European.

If one assumes that the genitive and the ablative originally constituted a single case in *-o-N* (thematic vowel plus nasal suffix), then according to Schmalstieg's hypothesis about monophthongizations in Indo-European, two sandhi variants should have developed—*-ō* and *-oN*. Moreover, it is entirely possible that the contamination of these two variants would have yielded a third variant—*-ōN*. I believe that the variant *-ō* is attested in such ablative forms as Skt. *vŕ̥kā-d* 'wolf', Lat. *lupō* (< *-ōd*), etc., that the variant *-oN* is seen as a genitive marker in Lat. *hominum* 'men' and OCS *jimenъ* 'names', and that the variant *-ōN* appears with this same function in forms like Gk. *lúkōn*, Skt. *vŕ̥kāṇām* 'wolves', etc. In other words, these sandhi variants became morphologized. The traditionally reconstructed ablative suffix *-ōd* results from a contamination of the ending *-ō* with the oblique marker *-T* (= *t* or *d*) (see below). Interestingly enough, Greek shows an adverbial suffix in *-ōs* (e.g. *kalôs* 'well') which is generally connected with the ablative singular (Buck 1933: 349). I feel that this suffix is a result of a contamination of the genitive-ablative (> ablative) suffix *-ō* with the genitive-ablative suffix in *-s*, rather than a specifically Greek contamination of *-ō* and an adverbial particle as Buck (1933: 349) suggests. Perhaps the Latin genitive plural ending *-ōrum* (< *-ōs*

+ *-oN*) shows this same *-ōs* element of the genitive-ablative in
contamination with the genitive-ablative suffix *-oN*.[3] My hypothesis regarding the nature of the *o*-stem ablative suffix also explains
the fact that "the vowel was *ō* in ordinary nominal declension alter-
nating with *ē* in adverbial forms (Lat. *facillumēd*)" (Burrow 1973:
233). Just as the *s*-suffix of the genitive-ablative showed variants
in *-es* and *-os*, so did the *N*-suffix show variants in *-eN* and *-oN*,
the latter two passing to *-ē* and *-ō*, respectively. Apparently the
ē-variant became largely specialized in adverbs at a later date.

However, the distribution of these genitive-ablative sandhi variants is actually more complicated than just indicated. The utilization of the variant *-oN* as an ablative marker is attested in the
Hittite ablative suffix *-anza*, a contamination of the endings *-oN*
(> Hitt. *-an*) and *-ts* (> Hitt. *-z* = *-/ts/*).[4] The importance of
this relic ending in support of my hypothesis is clear, since it
gives direct testimony to the use of the unaltered nasal suffix in
ablative function. Although "the source of the ending *-ēn* . . . is
uncertain" (Mann 1968: 107), perhaps Armenian attests this same
nasal suffix in ablative function in such pronominal forms as *y-inēn*,
ikēn, and *inēn*. However, the vocalic component of the suffix cannot
have been *-ē* or *-ō* originally if one assumes that it shows regular
Armenian phonological changes. Brugmann (1911: 417) says: "In dem
Ausgang *-ēn* vermutet Pedersen KZ. 38, 226 ein ähnliches Formans wie
in got. *meina*, *þeina*, so dass *inēn*, *kēn* auf dem Possessivum beruh-
ten"; but this is by no means a necessary assumption since contamination of some sort may be involved here, possibly a contamination
of an ablative marker in *-N* with "an originally independent particle (postposition)" *-ē*, which itself appears as an ablative suffix
in Armenian nouns (Godel 1975: 105).

It is clear that the nasal suffixes (and their reflexes) which
appear in the genitive and in the ablative are etymologically related, but the existence of an etymological relationship between the
nasal suffix of the historical accusative and that of the genitive-
ablative requires further justification. Benveniste (1971: 127)
concludes that "the genitive is the case that, between two nouns,
assumes for itself alone the function that in an utterance with a
personal verb falls to either the nominative or the accusative. All
the other uses of the genitive . . . are derived from this." Thus,
I believe that the genitive in *-N* has its origin in the old objective suffix *-N* having appeared in ambiguous constructions like *the
killing of the dragon* in order to indicate that *the dragon* is to be
understood as an object of *killing*. The old nominative in *-∅* was
used to mark *the dragon* as a subject here if that was the intended
meaning. I shall explain below how the historical genitive case

evolved from this situation. Hirt (1934: 100-103) describes numerous attested instances in which the genitive and the accusative
cases are confused and, as a result of these, argues that "der Geni-
tiv ursprünglich ein Akk. war" (1934: 101). Moreover, Kurylowicz
(1964: 184) also notes that in the historical dialects various
verbs show a "competition of the gen. with the acc." in taking objects: "E.g. in the RV the verb *man* 'to think of, remember' is construed with the acc. and (less frequently) with the gen. like
yajñásya 'the sacrifice', *te ávasaḥ* 'thy help', *eṣā́m* 'them'. In
Homer *klúō* and *akoúō* govern the gen. but also the acc. of the (inanimate) object. In Lat. *memini* (*commemini*, *recordari*) require,
like Greek *mimnḗskō*, either the acc. or the gen., this double construction spreading analogically also to *oblivisci*. In Goth. (and
similarly in other Germanic dialects) the verb 'to hear' (Goth.
hausjan) may govern not only the acc. but also the gen. In Slav.
both the gen. and the acc. are used with the verb 'to remember'."
The assumption that the accusative and the genitive derive from a
single case category naturally explains these data.

3.2   *-N* as a Marker of the Dative-Instrumental. It would seem
that the nasal suffixes found in the accusative, the genitive, and
the ablative derive originally from an objective case in *-N*. I
believe that the nasal suffix attested in the dative and the instrumental should be similarly analyzed. Schmalstieg (1977b: 127) argues that the accusative, dative, and instrumental cases all derive
from a common form in *-N*. In the *o*-stem class, two variant forms
would have arisen because of the preconsonantal monophthongization
of *-o-N*. He says that "the ending *-oN* is encountered . . . in the
following dative singular forms: Goth. *þam-ma*, Lith. *tam-ui*, OCS
tom-u 'that'. The Slavic *o*-stem dative singular ending (*grad-*)*u*
'(to the) city' represents a sporadic denasalization of word-final
-ǫ from *-om*, see Schmalstieg, 1971. The *-oN* is also attested in
the OCS instrumental singular (*grad-*)*omь* 'city' with a contamination
from the ending *-i*. The variant in *-ō* is represented in the Vedic
inst. sg. (*yajñ-*)*ā* 'sacrifice' (later transferred to the consonant
stems) and in the Lith. inst. sg. (*diev-*)*ù* 'god' (< *-úo* < *-ó*).
The variant in *-ō* is also represented in the following dative singular forms: Latin (*lup-*)*ō* [cf. Blümel 1972: 54-57--K.S.] and
(with contamination from the ending *-i*) Greek (*lúk-*)*ǭ*, Avestan
(*vəhrk-*)*āi*, Lith. (*vil̃k-*)*ui*, Sanskrit (*vṛk-*)*āya* 'wolf', although in
the Sanskrit form we may see the same particle *-ya* which we find in
the gen. sg. (*vṛk-*)*as-ya*." The original unity of the dative and the
instrumental cases, as well as their etymological relationship to
the ablative, is suggested by the fact that all three cases share a
common form in the dual number, although in some dialects a *bh-*

formant is attested (Skt. *vŕ̥kā-bhyām* 'two wolves'), while in others
a nasal suffix appears (OCS [dat.-inst.] *vlъkoma*, Lith. [dat.]
vilkám 'two wolves'). I believe that this nasal is the same one
attested in the singular of the dative, instrumental, and ablative.
It is interesting to note that the lengthened stem-vowel which Indo-
Iranian shows here may represent the preconsonantal sandhi variant
of the suffix *-oN* (> *-ō* > Skt. *-ā*). In the plural number the
dative and the ablative share a common form, again with *bh-* and *N-*
formants being variously attested (Skt. *vŕ̥kē-bhyas* 'wolves', *mātŕ̥-*
bhyas 'mothers', Lat. *nāvi-bus* 'ships', *equā-bus* 'horses'; OCS [dat.]
vlъko-mъ, Lith. [dat.] *vilká-m(u)s* 'wolves', OCS [dat.] *noštьmъ*,
Lith. [dat.] *naktĩms* 'nights'). Interestingly enough, Schmid (1973:
298) also maintains that an *-ō* serves as a base element for the
dative, instrumental, and ablative cases and that this form was extended by various suffixes to derive autonomous case morphemes.
However, he feels that the original function of the element was
"directive" (a state of affairs supposedly attested in the Old Hittite directive case in *-a*, cf. Starke 1977: 25-45 and Neu 1979:
186-187); and he posits no etymological connection between *-ō* and
forms in *-N*. A very strong indication of the original unity of the
dative-instrumental and the accusative is the continued existence in
the dialects of double accusative constructions, relics of the stage
of Indo-European when the uncontaminated nasal suffix served a much
wider functional role: Gk. *eirōtậs m' ónoma* 'you ask me my name',
hipposúnas se edídaksan 'they taught you the art of riding', cf.
Hirt 1934: 94-95 and Schmalstieg 1977b: 128. Likewise, the fact
that the accusative has in the dialects such secondary functions as
"acc. of direction (goal) after verbs of movement, both intransitive
and transitive," "acc. of temporal extension," and "acc. of spatial
extension," etc. (Kurylowicz 1964: 181-183) also implies that it,
along with the adverbial cases, derives from an original objective
which embraced a wide variety of functional roles.

In closing this section, I should point out that the identity of
the ablative and the genitive in the singular, and of the ablative
and the dative(-instrumental) in the non-singular has always been
a source of perplexity for Indo-Europeanists. For example, Hirt
(1934: 41-42) says: "Der Ablativ hat im Sing. im wesentlichen die
Form des Genitivs, im Plural die des Dativs. Das ist ausserordent-
lich auffallend und ganz unverständlich"; while Burrow (1973: 239)
similarly observes: "Anomalously the ablative which in the singular has mainly the same form as the genitive, has in the plural a
form identical with that of the dative." However, if one assumes
that all of these cases derive from a single category, then the

problem is easily resolved—one merely sees divergent differentia-
tions of this original case in the two numbers.

3.3   *-N as a Marker of the Locative. The nasal suffix of the old
objective case is also historically attested in the locative. For
example, it appears in such locative forms as Skt. *áśvāyām* 'mare'
and OP *schisman* 'this', cf. Gray 1932:   192.[5] "A similar element
-*i(n)* is found in Skt. and Av. loc. types like *a-sm-în*, *a-hm-i*,
a-hm-y-a, and in Homeric ablatives, instrumentals, and locatives
(both sing. and plur. without distinction of form) in -*phi(n)* < *-*bh*
-*i(n)*:   abl. sing. *melathróphin*, plur. *osteóphin*; instr. sing.
bíephin, plur. *theóphin*; loc. sing. *eskharóphin*, plur. *ikrióphin*.
Here, too, one must place Dor. *emín*, *tín*, Boeot. *hein* < **seɸin*,
Lesb. *ammi(n)*, *ummi(n)*, Attic *hēmîn*, *humîn*" (Gray 1932:   192-193).[6]
These forms may perhaps also show *-N* in contamination with other
elements, e.g. the suffix *-i*, with *-m* > -*n* in Sanskrit on analogy
with the endingless locative of the *n*-stems. A related locative
nasal suffix is perhaps seen in Hitt. *ketani* 'this' and Sanskrit adverbs like *idắnīm* 'now', *tēdắnīm* 'then', cf. Josephson 1967: 137-138.
Likewise, a similar construction is perhaps described by Brugmann
(1911:   181):   "Umbrisch. Neben *tote*, *Akeřunie* auch -*em*: *Acersoniem*,
totem-e (mit -*e(n)* 'in')."

   I am tempted to propose that the problematic Hittite adverbs in
-*an* show, at least in part (i.e. those with locative meaning), this
same nasal element (e.g. *dagan* 'at the bottom'). Kronasser (1966:
353-354) says that the "-*an* ist dreierlei Herkunft, dürfte aber als
ziemlich einheitliches Element empfunden worden sein: Zunächst
stammt es von *andan* mit Anhang, dann vom 1. sg. (*dagan*, *takšan*) und
schliesslich von *man* und m. E. jüngerem, *maḫḫan* 'als, wie' . . . ;
jenes geht wohl einfach auf **mom* zurück (wie lat. *quom*, *cum* 'als'
auf **kᴬᵘom* und *cum* 'mit' auf **k̂om*. . .)." Although he implies that
it was the endingless locative of the *n*-stems which generally provided the element (with the apparent reanalysis of -*n-Ø* as -*an*), I
would argue that there is no reason why an original locative in -*an*
cannot be assumed here. Indeed, Starke's assertion (1977:   171-172)
that the Hittite locative adverbs in -*an* can stand in apposition
with nouns in the locative case, implying the original locative
character of -*an*, strongly supports my proposal regarding the relationship between these Hittite forms and the Indo-European objective
case in *-N*, although Kammenhuber's criticisms (1979:   117-121) of
Starke's analysis demonstrate that it is by no means certain.
Starke (1977:   172-173) says: ". . . so liegt . . . bei *andan* É-*ri*,
kattan INA ᴱ*ḫalentu*, . . . eine Apposition vor, denn obwohl in der
Endung formal unterschieden, nehmen lok. Adverb und Lokativ dieselbe
semantische Position ein, was bedeutet, dass sie auch dieselbe di-

mensionale Funktion haben, was wiederum Voraussetzung für das Zu-
standekommen der Apposition ist. Die nähere Bestimmung der Apposition identifiziert sich nämlich mit dem Begriffsinhalt des Bezie-
hungswortes bezüglich der Angabe, die sich aus der Funktion seines
Kasus ableitet. Bei *labarnaš* LUGAL-*uš* ist 'König' identisch mit
'*labarna*' als Subjekt, bei ANA A.AB.BA KUR ^{URU}*Zalpuu̯a* (KBo XXII 2
Vs. 4) ist 'Land Zalpa' identisch mit 'Meer' als Zielangabe. Ebenso
verhält es sich mit *anda parna* und *andan É-ri*. Die Apposition ist
dem Beziehungswort beigeordnet und steht somit gleichrangig neben
ihm, was sich darin zeigt, dass die Aussage in keiner Weise ein-
geschränkt wird, wenn man das Beziehungswort weglässt." Starke
(1977: 174-175) further points out that similar constructions exist
in which "das lok. Adverb hinter dem Lokativ bzw. lok. Dativ steht.
So gibt es z.B. *karaitti piran* (B 300) . . . und LUGAL-*i piran* (B 301
und 302) . . . ." My proposal is also consonant with that of Szemerényi (1956: 62-66), who sees the alternation of -*a*/-*an* in these
forms as resulting from the development of sandhi variants of an
original demonstrative particle in *-*ŋ̥*, attested in Greek (*katá* <
*kṃt-ṃ). This nasal could very well be the vocalic alternate of the
locative suffix in *-*N*.

The Greek forms in -*phi*(*n*) also seem to attest to the original
identity of the ablative, instrumental, and locative cases. The
identity of these same cases has also been proposed by Houwink ten
Cate (1967), who, after showing "that in a number of Old Hittite
texts archaic forms in -*d* [probably the same dental element seen in
the ablative of various historical dialects--K.S.] functioning as
locatives may be found for . . . [the enclitic--K.S.] possessive
pronoun" (1967: 123), concludes that "in the use of one adverbial
ending for an instrumental and ablatival as well as locative function the enclitic possessive pronoun exhibits a characteristic archaism, which tends to show that the distinction between locative,
ablative, and instrumental case endings must have been a comparatively late phenomenon in the pronominal declension" (1967: 132).
The original etymological connection between the ablative and the
locative is also suggested by the fact that the ablative case residually retains a locative function in what has been termed "the locative ablative." Hirt (1934: 48-49) says: "Der Ablativ ist auch
in den westeuropäischen Sprachen verhältnismässig leicht zu erkennen.
Indessen hat der Ablativ frühzeitig und vielleicht schon in idg.
Zeit eine lokativische Bedeutung angenommen. Er steht vielfach auf
die Frage 'wo'." In support of his claim, Hirt (1934: 49) points
out that "die zahlreichen der Form nach deutlich ablativischen Adverbien wie l. *extrā* 'ausserhalb', *intrā* 'innerhalb', *infra*, g.
undarō, ai. *adharāt* 'unten' haben lok. Bedeutung." Similarly, "Auch

die Adverbien auf -*tos*, die ursprünglich ablativische Bedeutung
haben, zeigen lokativische" (1934: 49). The archaic nature of this
usage is strongly implied by the fact that "the Hitt. ablative sometimes denotes place where and time when" (Sturtevant 1932: 3).
Moreover, on the basis of both formal (their sharing the desinence
*-*i*, cf. dat. sg. *-*ōi*: Avest. *vəhrkāi*, Lith. *vilkui* 'wolf'; inst.
sg. *-*bhi*, *-*mi*: Hom. *theóphi* 'god', OCS *vlъkomь* 'wolf'; loc. sg.
*-*i*: Skt. *mánasi* 'mind', Lat. *homine* 'man') and semantic correspond-
ences, Kurylowicz (1964: 199) argues that "the *dat.* and the *instr.*
seem to have been originally secondary functions of the loc.," although I would see these parallels as resulting from their common
origin in the objective case. The complete formal identity in Hittite of the dative and the locative in -*i* further strengthens this
analysis of the original unity of these cases. Substantive evidence
also indicates the original unity of the locative and the genitive.
Because the genitive and the locative share a common form in the
dual number, Kurylowicz (1964: 200) concludes: "The paradigm of
the dual suggests an original identity of the gen. and the loc., i.e.
a prehistorical stage attested neither in the sing. (-*s*, -*i*) nor in
the plural (-*ōm*, -*su/*-*si*)." The original functional identity of the
two cases is perhaps suggested by the fact that the genitive has
also residually retained a secondary locative function, which Brugmann (1904: 438) describes as "Der Gen. von räumlichen und zeit-
lichen Begriffen." All in all, then, it would seem that Indo-European did possess an objective case in *-*N* which served as the basis
for the accusative, genitive, ablative, dative, instrumental, and
locative cases in later stages of the language and in the dialects.

3.4   The Origin of the Oblique Case. As time passed, Indo-European
added to its system of declension a number of other inflectional
elements—*-*s*, *-*i*, *-*T*, and *-*bh*—which generally came into competition with the objective suffix *-*N* in its oblique (non-accusative)
functions. Perhaps originating as adverbial particles of some sort,
cf. Markey 1979: 66, these new formants apparently did not completely replace the objective marker *-*N* in the oblique functions,
but rather served to increase the number of exponents a particular
case function possessed. Eventually certain of these elements became the primary exponents of particular cases (and numbers); but,
as has just been demonstrated, *-*N* or its reflexes continued in some
way or another to serve as markers of all the oblique cases into the
historical dialects, although the productivity of the suffix was
very limited in indicating a few of the cases. The ultimate result
of all of these developments was the creation of a language with a
great deal of inflectional polymorphy.

3.4.1 The Oblique Marker *-s. Because of its widespread occurrence
in oblique-case functions in the historical dialects, the suffix *-s
must have come into competition with *-N at an early date. I believe that at some stage of development, Indo-European came to possess the following nominal paradigm:

> nominative   *-∅, *-N (inanimate nouns only)
> accusative   *-N, *-∅ (inanimate nouns only)
> oblique   *-s, *-i (and probably *-T)

although the "accusative" suffix *-N continued to mark the oblique
case as well with regularity. A system similar to this one is actually found in Lydian, where "la flexion nominale présente un nomina-
tif en -s (en -a dans certains noms féminins en -a), un accusatif
en -n (écrit souvent -ν) et un cas oblique en -l" (Meillet and
Cohen 1952: 209); in Lydian "the oblique case ending. . . functions
as a locative . . . , as a dative . . . , and probably as a genitive"
(Sturtevant 1925: 70).

Traces of the original general oblique value of this *-s element
can be observed in various attested forms, especially in the pronominal system. This fact is, I believe, very important since there
is "a conserving force that is stronger in pronouns than anywhere
else, namely the force of habit. . . . When a pronoun or pronominal
paradigm has once been established, it often shows a marvelous per-
sistence of form, and except for the inevitable sound changes, may
remain unaltered for thousands of years" (Petersen 1932: 164-165).

Now in the demonstrative pronouns there appear three stem-formants
in *-s-: *-sm-, *-sy-, and *-s-. "The -sm- element. . . largely
remains, peculiar to the singular masculine and neuter dat., abl.,
and loc. cases" (Lane 1961: 471): "-sm-: sg. masc. and neut. dat.
Skt. tasmāi, Av. aētahmāi, Cret. ótīmi (= hó-tōi), Umb. esmei, . . .
OPruss. stesmu; abl. Skt. tasmāt, Av. aētahamāt; loc. Skt. tasmin,
Av. aētahmi, Umb. esme" (Lane 1961: 471). "The element -sy-, as
opposed to -sm-, is a peculiarity of the feminine singular forms,
and, in Indo-Iranian, particularly of the dative, ablative-genitive,
and locative" (Lane 1961: 473): "-sy-: sg. masc. and neut. gen.
Skt. tasya, Av. aētahe, Gk. toîo > toû, OIr. ái (< *esyo?), OPruss.
stesse (?); sg. fem. dat. tasyāi, Av. kahyāi-cit; (abl.-)gen. Skt.
tasyās, Av. aētaŋhā̊; Ir. ái (*esyās?); OPruss. stesses, -ssies,
-ssias(?); loc. Skt. tasyām, Av. kaŋhe" (Lane 1961: 471). "The
element -s- is not confined to the singular, but is characteristic
also of the genitive plural of all genders" (Lane 1961: 474):
"-s-: sg. fem. dat. Goth. þizai, OIcel. þeire, OE þǣre, OHG deru,
etc.; gen. Goth. þizōs, OIcel. þeirar, OE þǣre , OHG dera, etc.; pl.
masc. and neut. gen. Skt. tesām, Av. aētaēšąm, OPers. tyaišām; Umb.

erom, Goth. *þizē*, OHG *dero*, etc.; fem. gen. Skt. *tāsām*, Av. *yåŋhąm*,
Gk. *tā́ōn* > *tôn*, Lat. *is-tārum*, Osc. *eizazun-c*, Goth. *þizō*, OIcel.
þeira, OE *þāra*, etc. (= masc.); possibly also the locative plural
forms in *-su* (*-si*), masc.-neut. Skt. *teṣu*, Gk. *toîsi*, etc., fem.
Skt. *tāsu*, Gk. *têsi*, etc." (Lane 1961: 471). It is clear that
these three *s*-formants all serve to mark the various oblique cases,
and I believe that they suggest the existence of an original sigmatic oblique case. I see the form *-sy-* as deriving from a contamination of this original suffix *-s* and the oblique suffix *-i*, while
-sm- represents a similar contamination of *-s* and the objective
marker *-N*. These suffixes then became contaminated with other elements and lost their specifically desinential value in pronominal
declension after reanalysis as stem-formants.[7]

I believe that a contaminated suffix containing the ancient sigmatic oblique ending is attested as a desinence in nominal declension in both the genitive-locative dual and the locative plural. I
see the genitive-locative dual ending *-ous* (Skt. *vṛkayōs* 'two
wolves', *sūnōs* 'two sons', OCS *vlъku* 'two wolves'), cf. Brugmann
1904: 389-390, as consisting of the thematic vowel plus a contamination of the deictic particle *-u* or the dual suffix *-u* (attested,
e.g., in Skt. nom.-acc. *vṛkāu* 'two wolves', which alternates with
vṛkā)[8] and the oblique marker *-s*. Avest. *-ā̊* perhaps represents a
contamination of *-ō* (< *-oN*) and *-s*, cf. Brugmann 1911: 207.
The locative plural endings *-si* (Gk. *lúkoisi* 'wolves') and *-su*
(Skt. *vṛkēṣu*, OCS *vlъcěxъ* 'wolves') simply represent contaminations
of this ancient oblique marker and the oblique desinence *-i* and the
deictic particle *-u*, although it is possible that "the *s* can be
identified as the plural *s* which appears in other cases, to which
the further elements *i* and *u* are added in the two types" (Burrow
1973: 240).[9]

Before citing other case-forms where the oblique marker *-s*
appears, I should point out just how these contaminations came about.
I believe that they were motivated by the introduction of the nominative suffix *-s* into the system of declension. The appearance of
this suffix would have created an undesirable homophony between the
nominative and the oblique case in *-s*; and, thus, the sigmatic
oblique case began to renew itself. The contamination of *-s* with
-N was one way in which its autonomy was preserved. Since the accusative in *-N* retained much of its original general objective
value, it would not be unexpected that this element *-N* should become contaminated with *-s*. Likewise, the autonomy of the sigmatic
oblique case was also maintained by the contamination of *-s* with
the oblique suffix *-i* and the adverbial element *-u*.

Still, in nominal inflection the *s*-suffix is retained in uncontaminated form in the genitive(-ablative). In fact, I believe that the genitive in *-*s* and the nominative in *-*s* underwent a complete merger of form, as the identity of nominative and genitive in Hittite nouns like *attaš* 'father' demonstrates. The formal identity of the nominative and the genitive in *-*s* in Indo-European has long been recognized: "Dem Nominativsuffix (Sg.) ähnelt auffälligerweise das Suffix des Genitivs Sg., das man regelmässig in der Gestalt *s/es/os* rekonstruiert. Das ursprüngliche Identität der beiden Suffixe wurde bereits im J. 1902 von N. v. Wijk überzeugend nachgewiesen. Seine Argumente gelten im grossen und ganzen noch heute" (Erhart 1970: 114). Lehmann (1958: 192) explains further: "Since accent alone differentiated the etymon of the genitive from that of the nominative, there would be no segmental basis for distinguishing between the two forms. And because in pre-Indo-European the occurrence of the main accent was syntactically conditioned, morphologically there was no distinction between the etyma of the nominative and the genitive." However, what I am suggesting is that the identity of the nominative and the genitive cases in *-*s* was not original, but developed from syncretism of the cases. It was when the Pre-Indo-European syntactically conditioned accent became morphologically conditioned in Proto-Indo-European, cf. Lehmann 1958: 192-195, that a distinction between the two reappeared. Such a merger of cases is not unusual; indeed, the historical dialects attest to many such mergers. Moreover, what Wandruszka (1969: 226) calls "paradigmatische Polysemie," "die Verwendung ein und derselben [inflectional--K.S.] Form in verschiedenen Funktionen" (1969: 218), is a common property of inflectional languages. For example, in Latin the ending *-ae* serves as the marker of the genitive singular, the dative singular, and the nominative plural, cf. *rōs-ae* 'rose' (Wandruszka 1969: 226).

Despite the existence of the contaminations noted above, it would seem that from the time of the introduction of the nominative ending *-*s*, the dative, instrumental, and, to a lesser extent, locative functions of the old oblique-case suffix *-*s* began to be transferred to other suffixes in order to minimize ambiguity so that only in the genitive(-ablative) is *-*s* generally retained. However, the problem remains: why did the genitive(-ablative) function alone retain *-*s* as a primary exponent and thereby undergo merger with the innovative nominative in *-*s*?

I would suggest that the retention of the suffix *-*s* in the genitive(-ablative) function is a result of the fact that the genitive bore a natural functional affinity to the nominative, which exerted an analogical influence on it. The nature of this close relation-

ship is tied up with the origin of the genitive case itself. Earlier
I indicated that in a construction like *the killing of the dragon*,
the dragon was originally marked by the objective suffix *-N* when
it was understood as an object and by the nominative suffix *-∅*
when it was understood as a subject. After the oblique case arose,
-s, too, at times was used to mark *the dragon* as an object of *killing*. Now when the new nominative suffix in *-s* began to become generalized at the expense of *-∅*, it was used to mark *the dragon* as a
subject of *killing*. But the occurrence of an *-s* with both values
resulted in a surface ambiguity which led to the reinterpretation
of the nominative suffix *-s* here as an occurrence of the oblique
ending *-s*. It was at this point that the classic Indo-European
genitive case, i.e. the case that "basically results from the process of converting a sentence into a nominal . . . , the genitive
representing a kind of neutralization of the nominative/accusative
distinction found in the underlying sentence" (Fillmore 1968: 8),
became fully developed. On analogy with the oblique (> genitive)
suffix *-s*, the objective (> genitive) marker *-N* could also now
be affixed to *the dragon* in its subjective sense. Thus, this natural parallelism of function between the nominative and the historically attested subjective genitive construction, cf. Brugmann 1904:
439-440, contributed to the retention of *-s* in the genitive, since
speakers of Indo-European would have associated the two cases.

Other parallels also exist between the function of the genitive
and the function of the nominative. For example, although develop-
ing somewhat later but nevertheless reinforcing the close relationship which speakers felt between the two cases is the use of the
genitive (in its partitive function) to serve as the subject of a
sentence. As Brugmann (1904: 626) says: "Bei den 3. Personen kann
statt des Nominativs auch ein partiver Gen. das Subjekt bilden, z.B.
av. *kaṯ tā̆ paθā̆ fraᵧǫn pasvǫm vā staorǫm vā narǫm vā nā̆ⁱrinǫm*
'dürfen diese Pfade betreten Kleinvieh oder Zugvieh, Männer oder
Frauen?'." Of course, the *-s* genitive was not distinctively singular at this time. Another parallel between the two cases is described by Lehmann (1958: 199): there exists in Hittite an ancient
construction which shows "the apparent use . . . of some genitives
to indicate subjects, as described by Friedrich, *Hethitisches Elementarbuch* 1.69. Among the examples given by Friedrich is *u̯aš̑tulaš̑*
'of sin' (< *u̯aš̑tul* 'sin'), which may have the meaning 'sinner'. In
form *u̯aš̑tulaš̑* is genitive; in meaning it corresponds to a nominative." Friedrich (1974: 123) characterizes it as an elliptical
construction: "Eine sehr beliebte Konstruktion im Hethitischen ist
der Ausdruck 'der des . . . , das des . . .' zur Umschreibung eines
anderen Nomens." Likewise, there is a "similar Hittite use of geni-

tives of infinitives, e.g. *naḫḫuuaš* 'one who shows reverence'"
(Lehmann 1958: 199). These examples, then, demonstrate the close
functional relationship between the nominative and the genitive—a
fact which led to the retention of the oblique ending *-s*, homophonous with the suffix *-s* of the nominative case, in the genitive.

I would like to suggest that the oblique suffix *-s* also exists
in uncontaminated form as a desinence in the suffix *-s* which appears
in the dative case of the personal pronouns attested in Gothic and
other Germanic languages—a formation about which Schmidt (1978:
135) says: "Die germ. Dat.-Formen got. *mis*, *þus*, *sis*, ahd. *mir*,
dir < germ. **mez*, **þuz* oder **þez* (**sez* ist nur gotonord. und wohl
*mez, **þuz* nachgebildet) sind unerklärt." In other words, I see
these pronominal forms as relics of a very early system of declension. Although this suffix appears to be limited to dative function
here, it should be emphasized that in Gothic (and early Germanic)
"the dative also discharges the functions of the old ablative, instrumental, and locative" (Wright and Sayce 1968: 186); and thus
its preservation in Germanic has perhaps been motivated by the fact
that the attested dative largely performs the functions of the original oblique suffix *-s*. It is possible that the oblique suffix
-s is similarly attested in the Umbrian dative reflexive pronoun
seso, which may very well derive from **ses-so*, with **-so* representing a deictic particle, cf. Hirt 1927: 13-14, affixed to an original oblique case-form **ses*.

3.4.2 The Oblique Marker *-i*. Another element, *-i*, perhaps etymologically related to the deictic particle of the 'here and now',
cf. Watkins 1962: 102, also came into competition with the old objective suffix *-N* in its oblique functions at a very early date.
This ending appears most conspicuously in nominal declension as a
marker of the dative (e.g. dat. sg. **-ōi*, a contamination of **-ō* <
*-oN and **-i*: Avest. *vəhrkāi*, Lith. *viĺkui*, OHG *wolfe* 'wolf', Gk.
híppō 'horse'), the instrumental (e.g. inst. sg. **-mi*, a contamination of **-N* and **-i*: OCS *vlъkomь* 'wolf', Lith. *naktimì* 'night';
*-bhi, a contamination of **-bh* and **-i*: Hom. *theóphi* 'god', Armen.
gailov 'wolf'), and the locative (e.g. loc. sg. **-i*: Skt. *śúni*,
Gk. *kuní* 'dog', Lat. *homine* 'man'). The appearance of **-i* in Hom.
-phi(n) also guarantees its use as an ablative indicator. The fact
that in Hittite the dative and the locative share a common form in
-i demonstrates that this suffix in itself served a number of different functions in Indo-European.

I would also like to propose that the originally oblique suffix
-i is historically attested with regularity as a marker of the
genitive(-ablative) in nominal declension. Its retention in this

function into the historical period would be expected since there
exists a universal linguistic tendency for the genitive and the locative (whose primary exponent was *-i in later stages of the language) to share a common form—a situation motivated by the close
semantic and syntactic relationship among existential, locative, and
possessive constructions, cf. Lyons 1971: 388-395 and Clark 1978.

I believe that the Indo-European genitive (< oblique) marker *-i
is attested regularly in the o-stem nominal class in the suffix
traditionally reconstructed as *-$si̯o$ (Skt. $vŕ̥kasya$, Avest. $vəhrkahe$,
Hom. $lúkoio$ [< *-o-$si̯o$], Armen. $gailoy$ 'wolf', and perhaps Faliscan
$kaisíosio$ 'Kaisius'), which, of course, represents a contamination
of the oblique markers *-s and *-i with the thematic vowel. As I
indicated earlier, the suffix *-$si̯$- is attested in pronominal declension as an oblique stem-formant; and in the genitive (singular)
it, too, appears with an affixed *-o (Skt. $tásya$, Hom. $toîo$ 'his',[10]
Avest. ahe 'of this', OIr. $ái$ 'of the'). This same desinence *-i
in genitive function is also perhaps seen in the y-element of the
o-stem genitive-locative dual: Skt. $vŕ̥kayōs$, Avest. $vəhrkayå̊$
(< *-o-$i̯$-ous) 'two wolves', cf. pronominal forms like Skt. $táyōs$,
Avest. $ayå̊$, OCS $toju$. Tocharian clearly attests a gentive formation
in *-i. Petersen (1939: 91-92) says: "The genitives in -i look as
though they were phonetic variants of those in -e, but there is a
prohibitive reason against such a supposition in the domain of their
occurrence. Except for a number of foreign proper names only the
nouns of relationship are found with this ending: $pācri$, $mācri$, and
$pracri$ from $pācar$, $mācar$, and $pracar$. This marks the -i as different from the -e which has been traced to the IE i-stems and was al-
most confined to the feminine gender. Nor can it be the remnant of
the IE genitive suffix -es, since this combination has been seen to
disappear completely everywhere else." Although Petersen sees this
formation as an analogical one, suggesting that "it is the -i of the
enclitic pronominal forms $ñi$ 'mei, mihi, me' and ci 'tui, tibi, te',
which come from IE *moi and *toi, so that their -i is unaccented IE
-oi," this is by no means a necessary conclusion. I see this Tocharian ending as an analogical extension of an ancient o-stem genitive (< oblique) desinence *-o-i. Of course, Petersen is making
his comments in regard to the A dialect of Tocharian (East Tocharian);
however, the more recently investigated Tocharian B dialect (West
Tocharian) shows a similar formation. Thus, Krause and Thomas (1960:
105) note that the genitive singular suffix "-i tritt in beiden Dialekten bei Verwandtschaftsnamen auf -r auf: A $pācri$ = B $pātri$ (N. A
$pācar$, B $pācer$); entsprechend A $mācri$ [B $mātri$], $pracri$ [$protri$]. . . .
Die Genitivendung -i findet sich in beiden Dialekten ferner in einer
Reihe von fremden Personnamen, z.B. B $Mahākāśyapi$ (N. -e) [A $Kāśyapi$,

N. *Kā́śyap*]. . . ." Krause and Thomas (1960: 59) also point out
that one etymological source of AB *-i* is **-oi*, as in the case of
"Toch. *-i* aus idg. *-oi* in der Endung des N. Pl. der Deklinations-
klasse V wie A *koñi* [B *kauñi*] 'Tage'."

I further believe that the problematic Gothic genitive plural suffix *-ē* derives from an *o*-stem genitive formation in **-i*. Now in
Germanic the attested *o*-stem genitive singular is in **-e-so* in both
nouns (Go. *wulfis*, OHG *wolfes* 'wolf') and pronouns (Go. *hvis* , OHG
hwes 'which'), i.e. **-so* with *e*-grade ablaut of the stem-vowel. This
same formation is also found in pronominal declension in Slavic (OCS
česo 'whose') and Greek (*téo* < **teso*). Old Prussian may show **-o-ε̄o*
in such forms as *deiwas* 'God', although this genitive suffix may be
derived also from **-o-si̯o* (Dyen 1974: 131). According to Krause
and Thomas (1960: 104), the West Tocharian genitive singular ending
-ntse shows the suffix **-so* in contamination with the Tocharian oblique case-marker **-m̥* (or perhaps the genitive [< objective] marker
*-N, cf. Schmalstieg 1977b: 124). But since the Baltic and Tocharian evidence can be interpreted in various ways, it may be, as Dyen
(1974: 132) proposes, that "the extreme restriction on the distribution of **-e-so* would suggest that the analogical transfer to nouns
is an event that affected only Proto-Germanic and perhaps followed
the transfer from the interrogative stems to demonstrative stems.
It seems reasonable to conclude that it is much less likely that **-so*
was a noun ending in PIE than that **-si̯o* was. It follows that in
assigning **-so* as a noun ending in the *o*-inflection to Proto-Indo-
European, Brugmann has been perhaps too hasty." However, as my
analysis of Indo-European nominal inflection so far has demonstrated,
I tend to view the Indo-European inflectional system as much more
fluid than those systems attested in the historical dialects themselves; thus, such statements implying an originally strict comple-
mentary distribution of suffixes in Indo-European which was altered
only later through analogical processes are, I believe, invalid assumptions.

According to the most widely held traditional theory, the Germanic
languages attest two *o*-stem formations in the genitive plural. "All
NWGmc. gen. pl. go back to *-õm*, e.g., ON OE *daga* (*ulfa*, *wulfa*), OS
wulfo, OHG *wolfo*. . . . In Gothic, *-ō* < **-õm* appears only in *ā*-stems
and, doubtless under their influence, in feminine *n*-stems: *gibō*,
tuggōnō" (Prokosch 1939: 240). This is the same ending **-ōN* which
serves generally in the other Indo-European dialects as the source
of the genitive plural suffix of the *o*-stems (and other classes),
cf. Gk. *lúkōn* 'wolves'. However, it is frequently assumed that "a
variant *e*-grade of this formation appears in Gothic only" (Burrow
1973: 240), *wulfē* < **-ẽN*, although many other theories concerning

the origin of the Gothic suffix exist.[11]   But what I would like to
suggest is that the Gothic ending derives from an original genitive
formation in *-o-i, which passed to *-ē according to the theory of
monophthongizations described earlier. This long-vowel desinence
would have passed to *-ǣ in Proto-Germanic and then to -ē in Gothic.
Of course, "Prim. Indg. long vowels, or those which became final in
prim. Germanic . . . , became shortened in polysyllabic words, when
the vowels in question originally had the 'broken' accent, but remained unshortened when they originally had the 'slurred' accent"
(Wright and Sayce 1968: 37). The preservation of length in the
Gothic suffix is simply a result of the fact that the form in -ē
also had the circumflex accent characteristic of the genitive plural,
just as "the preservation of the final -ē in adverbs with the suffix
-drē is also due to the vowel having had originally the 'slurred'
accent" (Wright and Sayce 1968: 38). It may perhaps be the case
that this form in *-ē became contaminated with the suffix *-N in the
late stages of Proto-Indo-European or even in Proto-Germanic, yielding *-ēN; but because of the loss of the nasal in this environment
in early Germanic, such a possibility can only be noted. The extension of the suffix -ē to other stem-classes can be explained in
rather simple terms within the context of this proposal: "IE -ā-om
> Gmc. -ōm would be apt to resist the spread of the ending -ē; in
the other classes, -om would have disappeared in Germanic, and the
resulting forms without ending (Go. guman- etc.) add -ē in Gothic,
-ō elsewhere" (Prokosch 1939: 240).

   The use of the genitive suffix -i in early Germanic is perhaps seen
in the Runic inscription on the gold ring of Bucharest: gutaniowi
hailag. Must (1952: 220-221) believes "that the first word is to be
taken as gutani 'of the Goths'," showing "the ending -ī for the genitive plural." "Although this incription . . . has not yet been
definitely interpreted," he feels that this -i constitutes the ancient i-stem genitive plural, which has been analogically extended.
However, his assumption that the vowel is long is not necessary.
Prokosch (1939: 134) says of vowels in final unaccented syllables:
"In Norse, early Runic retains i u after long as well as short syllables. . . ." Therefore, the vowel here may be an original short
one.

   I would like to propose further that an o-stem genitive formation
in *-i is also attested in Italo-Celtic. Simply, according to
Schmalstieg's theory of monophthongizations, the Indo-European phonological sequence *-ei passed to *-ī in preconsonantal position. This
*-ī would yield -ī in Italic (Lat. gen. sg. lupī 'wolf') and Celtic
(OIr. gen. sg. fir < *u̯irī 'man', Gaul. Segomari 'Segomaros'). Thus,
this genitive construction is exactly the same as the one which was

posited for Gothic, except that the stem is formed in *-e. However, since Italic and Celtic show the suffix in singular function, it is not surprising that this stem-variant would be attested here.[12]

The only apparent problem in the analysis involves the posited variability in the number-specification of the suffix *-i. But this is really no problem at all because the emergence of a specifically non-singular inflectional category was a late development in Indo-European. Indeed, as I pointed out earlier, the Hittite genitive endings -aš and -an appear in both the singular and the plural. I thus believe that the difference in the distribution of the suffix *-i in the various dialects is the result of the same inherent alternation in usage.

Although he admits that other analyses are possible, Schmalstieg (1980: 69-71) gives "a few examples where the etymological *-y has been retained in some forms which we term accusative," e.g., "in Old Irish the accusative singular of ben 'woman' in the oldest texts is bein, but according to Thurneysen, 1946: 184, from the time of the Würzburg glosses on the dative form mnaí is used for the accusative. It is usually stated that the accusative singular form mnaí is formed by analogy with the dative singular . . . , but this does not seem to be a necessary assumption." However, if this and the other forms he cites are indeed etymological accusatives, I believe that their rarity implies that *-i was, at best, used only sporadically in this function. Still, this means that the competition between *-N and *-i was not completely limited to the oblique cases.

3.4.3   The Oblique Marker *-T. The element *-T is largely confined to the ablative case of the o-stem nouns in the historical dialects, cf. Skt. vŕkād, etc. As I indicated earlier, *-T is seen here in contamination with the preconsonantal sandhi variant of the originally objective formation *-o-N. Hittite possesses an ablative suffix -(a)z (= -/(a)ts/), which is probably etymologically related to the suffix *-tos from which ablatival adverbs are formed in other Indo-European languages (e.g. Skt. mukhatás 'from the mouth', Lat. funditus 'from the bottom', Gk. ektós 'outside'). I believe that these two suffixes show the ending *-T in contamination with the old oblique (> genitive-ablative) ending *-(e/o)s. However, although both desinences represent similarly contaminated forms, it is possible that their existence is a result of parallel but independent processes. In this regard Schmid (1973: 300) says: "Wenn nun aber *-tos sich zerlegen lässt in *t + os, dann ist grundsätzlich auch mit der Möglichkeit zu rechnen, dass es auch ein *t + s gibt, da bei den Konsonantstämmen vereinzelt auch ein blosses -s als alte Genitivform nachweisbar ist. . . . Damit bietet sich die Möglichkeit an,

den hethitischen Ablativ auf -az auf *t + s zurückzuführen, ohne
dass man mit dem in der Tat unwahrscheinlichen Ablaut -tos/-ts rechnen muss. Das wäre dann eine hethitische Neubildung, die in der
Übernahme des Suffixes -tos in das Nominalparadigma im Alt- und
Mittelindischen eine Parallel, aber keinen Verwandten hätte." That
*-T originally served a more general oblique function than the indi-
cation of the ablative case is demonstrated by its widespread occurrence in the instrumental (singular and plural) of Hittite (e.g.
uttan-it 'thing, word') and in the genitive (singular) of Tocharian
B (-ntse, -m̥tse), cf. Schmalstieg 1980: 72.[13] As noted earlier,
Houwink ten Cate (1967) has identified in Old Hittite texts instances
of *-T marking the locative case in enclitic possessive pronouns,
e.g. "a-u-ri-iš-mi-it 'in your' (plur.) or 'in their watchtower'"
(1967: 124). Moreover, Schmid (1973: 300) posits a "hethitischen
Kasusendung -t [which, according to him, had an original directive
value--K.S.], die man auch in heth. ket 'hier(her)' zum Pronominalstamm ka- mit Dat.-Lok. keti (apeti, edi) feststellen kann." This
desinance -ti, which Schmid (1973: 299) connects with the suffix in
forms like Skt. á-ti, Gk. é-ti, Avest. ai-ti, etc., may represent a
contamination of the oblique markers *-T and *-i. I find it interesting that Hittite demonstrative pronouns show *-T in other oblique
cases as well, i.e. gen. sg. -etaš, gen. pl. -enzan, dat.-loc. sg.
also -etani, dat.-loc. pl. -etaš, abl. sg. -ez and -etaz, abl. pl.
-ez, inst. sg. and pl. -(i)t, cf. Friedrich 1974: 66. Although the
dental suffix is contaminated with other elements here, e.g. the
genitive ending -aš, its general oblique signification stands out
clearly. The widespread appearance of *-T in the dialects, along
with its normally limited but varied distribution and its non-productive character in all dialects except Hittite,[14] strongly implies
that it was once a commonly used suffix whose occurrence was re-
stricted only in the later stages of Indo-European and in the dialects, where it generally became a relic form, except in the ablative.

3.4.4   The Oblique Marker *-bh. An oblique inflectional element
*-bh also apparently existed in Indo-European. However, because its
distribution in nominal declension is limited to only certain dialects and because its function in these dialects differs significantly from one to the other, it is probably true that *-bh was a
rather late addition to the system of nominal inflection. In Indo-
Iranian *-bh appears as an indicator of the instrumental plural
(Skt. -bhis, Avest. -bĭš, OPers. -biš), the dative and ablative
plural (Skt. -bhyas, Avest. -byō), and the dative, ablative, and instrumental dual (Skt. -bhyām, Avest. -bya, OPers. -biyā), while

Homeric Greek attests *-phi(n)* as a marker of the ablative, instrumental and locative in both the singular and plural numbers. Armenian shows the ending *-b* (*-w* in postvocalic position) in the instrumental singular and *-bkh* (*-wkh* in postvocalic position) in the
instrumental plural. In the Italic and Celtic groups, reflexes of
-bh serve generally in the plural function of certain oblique cases,
although traces of their use in the dual are exemplified in Irish
(Lat. dat.-abl. pl. *-bus*, Osc. dat.-abl. pl. *-fs*, OIr. dat. pl. *-b*,
OIr. dat. du. *-b*). Because *-bh* is attested in the dative, instrumental, ablative, and locative cases, its original basically oblique
value is clear, although it seems generally to be contaminated with
other oblique suffixes, especially *-i*. Its failure to mark the
genitive case may be a result of the fact that the genitive had
largely become autonomous from the other oblique cases at about the
time when this element was introduced into the language. What is
very interesting about the suffix *-bh* is that the Germanic, Baltic,
Slavic, Tocharian, and Anatolian groups do not attest it as an inflectional element in nouns, but instead show another suffix where
-bh appears in the dialects already cited, e.g. *-N* in Baltic,
Slavic, and Germanic. However, as Markey (1979: 65-66) points out:
"Languages that elsewhere have only forms with *-m-* have *-bh-* in the
dative singular of the second person pronoun: OCS *te-bĕ*, OPr. *te-
bbei* beside Skt. *tú-bhya(m)*, GAv. *tai-byā̆*, Lat. *tibī̄*, Umbr. *te-fe*
and cf. Lat. *sibī̄* and *nōbī̄s*, *vōbī̄s*. In addition to implementation
as a case marker in both nominal and pronominal paradigms, it occurs
as an adverbial formant where the notions of directionality it con-
veys as a case marker are correlated with those of time. The obvious
examples are Lat. *ubi* and *ibi* = 'where : when' and 'there : then'
respectively. We can derive *ubī̄* from *$*k^w o$-bhei*, cf. Hitt. *ku-wa-pi*
= *kwapi* 'where, when' and see the discussion in Kronasser (1966:
348). . . . In Gothic alone of the Germanic dialects, *-bh-* forms
adverbs of manner, e.g. *bairhtaba*, *manwuba*, where Goth. *-ba* is generally regarded as a remnant of a case (inst. ?) marker. If so,
this vitiates postulation of a dialectal distinction between *-bh-*
and *-m-* within Indo-European. Moreover, the thesis that *-bh-* was
reserved for a set of functions from which *-m-* was excluded and vice
versa is untenable: the hypothesized original restriction of *-m-* to
the instrumental is, of course, invalidated by Armenian." In addition, I have proposed (1977) that *-bh(i)* is also to be found in
Tocharian, specifically in the Tocharian A additive particle *-pi*.
What all of this seems to imply is that an original deictic particle
-bh, "which subsequently received regularized paradigmatic assign-
ment (in the immediately pre-dialectal period)" (Markey 1979: 66),
came into competition with other oblique case markers. "In some

dialects, -*bh*- was extended at the expense of -*m*- [and *-*i* in uncontaminated form--K.S.], while in others the reverse was true"
(Markey 1979: 66). That is, because *-*bh* never really became a
fully integrated part of the inflectional system before the distin-
tegration of the Indo-European speech community, it was replaced by
older forms.

3.5   The Origin of the Vocative Case. A number of other important changes occurred in the Indo-European declensional system at
about the same time as the appearance of the oblique case. One such
change involved the formal separation of the nominative and the
vocative cases in the animate nouns. In the *o*-stem class, there
developed a qualitative difference in the stem vocalism of the two
case-forms (nominative = *o*, vocative = *e*): Gk. *lúkos* 'wolf', *lúke*
'O, wolf' ; Lat. *lupus* 'wolf', *lupe* 'O, wolf'; OCS *vlъkъ* 'wolf',
vlъče 'O, wolf'. Although this difference may have indeed been the
result of some sort of accentual change, as is so often suggested,
another explanation lies within the realm of possibility. Simply,
in contemporary phonological theory, it is recognized that the difference between the vowels *o* and *e* is a function of the phonological
feature "back" (Chomsky and Halle 1968: 304-306). That is, in the
production of *o*, the tongue is more retracted than in the articulation of *e*. However, under conditions of increased pitch, which are
to be expected in the rising intonation of the vocative, the vowel
o is rather significantly fronted (Parmenter, Treviño, and Bevans
1933: 77). Thus, it may have happened that these fronted allophones of /o/ were extremely close phonetically to some of the retracted allophones of /e/ and that a merger of these phone-types
eventually took place in this particular morphological environment.
This natural acoustic effect was then morphologized as an indicator
of the vocative function in the animate *o*-stems.

It should be pointed out that I believe the development of the
complicated system of vowel gradation, or ablaut, so important in
late Indo-European and the dialects, to have been very gradual, with
the ultimate origins of this morphological device stemming from a
number of separate linguistic changes (including accentual altera-
tions) whose results were eventually assimilated into a unified
scheme, cf. also Shields 1976, 1979d, Forthcoming a, and Forthcoming
b.

A more complicated problem concerning the origin of vocative formations is seen in the animate *i*- and *u*-stems, which have vocative
terminations in *-*ei* (*-*oi*) (e.g. Skt. *ávē* 'O, sheep', Avest. *ažē*
'O, serpent', Lith. *naktiẽ*, OCS *nošti* 'O, night') and *-*eu* (*-*ou*)
(e.g. Skt. *sū́nō*, Lith. *sū́naũ*, OCS *synu* 'O, son') as opposed to ori-

ginal nominatives in *-i-∅ and *-u-∅. Instead of explaining such
formations as resulting from very complicated accentual changes, I
would suggest that the vocative marker *-e of the o-stems was segmented as a special desinence of the vocative function and transferred to the i- and u-stems. Since this vocalic marker immediately followed the final consonant of the stem in the o-stem class, it
was analogically inserted into this position in the i- and o-stem
declensions. "Indirect evidence" also exists for animate i- and u
-stem vocatives in *-∅, i.e. *-i-∅ and *-u-∅ (Kurylowicz 1964: 198-
199), which are relic formations that attest to the original unity
of the nominative and the vocative in *-∅ and which derived their
specifically vocative function after the introduction of *-s as a
nominative marker. The *-e/*-o alternation found in the i- and u-
stem vocatives was probably motivated by a functional confusion of
the o-stem nominative and vocative forms, a confusion still attested
in the oldest of the historical languages, cf. Brugmann 1904:   445.
This stem-structure in *-e- (*-o-) was assimilated into the gradually emerging ablaut system of Indo-European and thereby came to
serve as the basis for a number of other case-constructions, e.g.
i- and u-stem nominative plurals. Before many such ablaut alternations acquired their characteristic morphological significance,
they merely constituted variant means of stem-formation.

In the case of the l-, r-, m-, n-, and s-stems, the nominative
came to differ from the corresponding vocative perhaps at a somewhat
later date by what is generally termed lengthened-grade ablaut: Gk.
kúōn 'dog', kúon 'O, dog'; Gk. mḗtēr 'mother', mêter 'O, mother';
Skt. durmanā́s 'troubled one', dúrmanas 'O, troubled one'; Skt. dā́tā
'giver', dā́tar 'O, giver'. Again, the traditional explanation concerning the origin of this quantitative difference involves the
operation of accent; but another interpretation is possible. According to Schmalstieg's theory of monophthongizations, *e + r, l, m, n
> *ē in preconsonantal position and *o + r, l, m, n > *ō in pre-
consonantal position. Thus, early Indo-European *pəter 'father'
became *pətē (Skt. pitā́, Avest. ptā) before a word-initial consonant and remained as *pəter (Skt. pítar, Avest. ptar, Gk. páter) before a word-initial vowel. Schmalstieg (1974c: 188) maintains
that the new form assumed the primary function of the nominative,
"whereas the secondary function, the vocative case, was retained by
the older form phonologically." The frequently reconstructed nominative form *pətḗr (Gk. patḗr, Lat. pater) merely shows an analogical restoration of the final resonant by means of a contamination
of the two variant stems. Also through analogy the long vowel was
introduced into the s-stems as a nominative marker (Skt. durmanā́s
'troubled one', Gk. dusmenḗs 'ill-disposed one', Avest. dušmanā̊

'one thinking evil'; Skt. $uṣā́s$, Gk. $ē\acute{o}s$ 'dawn'). I believe that
this analogical lengthening occurred after the introduction of *-s
as a marker of the nominative case, specializing *-∅ with or without
vocalic change in the secondary vocative function in the animate
nouns of all declensions except those with the naturally occurring
long vowel (which continued to show a nominative in *-∅) and the
s-stems. Since the phonetic sequence *-s-s was an impossible one in
the Indo-European of this era (Brugmann 1930: 812-813), the s-stems
adopted the long vowel in order to integrate themselves into the
existing system of animate nouns, which clearly indicated the nominative by means of the *-∅ termination in conjunction with vocalic
lengthening in the stem or by means of the suffix *-s, and the vocative by means of the *-∅ termination alone. Neuter nouns of all
declensions made no such differentiation between nominative and
vocative because of the rarity of these nouns in the vocative function. It should be emphasized again that at this point in time
Indo-European had no $ā$-stem nouns, although nouns in *-$ă$ did exist.
The archaic nature of attested a-stem forms (e.g. Gk. $n\acute{u}mpha$ 'nymph',
OCS $ženo$ 'woman') is demonstrated by the fact that in Greek and
Latin (where they function as nominatives and vocatives, thus suggesting the original unity of the two cases) and in Slavic (where
they function only as vocatives), they show the relic ending *-∅
without any vocalic change, cf. i-stem vocatives in *-i-∅. But because of lack of evidence resulting from the assimilation of a-stems
to the relatively recent $ā$-stems, the original nature of the Indo-
European a-stem vocative formation is impossible to ascertain.

3.6   The Origin of the Nominative Singular Animate Ending *-s.
Another addition to the inflectional system which I have referred
to a number of times was the nominative marker *-s, which came to
replace the older desinence *-∅ in certain animate stem-classes.
However, I believe that before the origin of this suffix can be considered fully, an investigation of the nature of the concordial
system of early Indo-European must be undertaken.

3.6.1   Concord in Early Indo-European. Since Indo-European was
most probably in its very earliest stages an isolating language,
grammatical agreement, or concord, among the various elements of
the sentence had a specific origin within the language as it developed its inflectional system. It would seem that concord primarily
appeared during the time when Indo-European was an ergative language and that it manifested itself especially within the noun
phrase because the items of which it is composed together represent
a highly integrated syntactic unit. Thus, the close relationship

which exists between a noun and its adjectival modifier(s) is crucial in the emergence of a concordial system. Since the noun and its modifier are placed not only in close "spatial" relationship but also in a close functional and structural relationship, it is natural for the structurally subordinate adjective to adopt the termination of the noun it modifies, cf. Kurylowicz 1964: 217.

Concord of this type, which Fodor (1959: 34) calls "assonance-like motion," originating through the basically analogical process just described, is not unknown in the development of the various historical Indo-European languages. Fodor (1959: 35), who also ascribes this type of concordial system to early Indo-European, notes its development "in the inflection of the post-positive article in Slavonic languages," specifically in Bulgarian and northern Russian dialects. In early Indo-European, then, the originally invariable adjective came to adopt the ending *-N in those instances where the noun which it modified was terminated in this element, and likewise the endings *-$\emptyset$ or *-r when the modified noun showed these suffixes. This type of concordial government within the noun phrase was carried over into the nominative-accusative stage of Indo-European so that the occurrence of nominal endings (*-$\emptyset$ and *-N) on the adjective automatically extended the indication of the nominal gender category to the adjective as well.

That the adjective was originally invariable does not imply that its structure was substantially different from that of the noun. Indeed, it was always subject to the same phonological constraints as the noun. Moreover, it is probably true that the Indo-European noun, adjective, and verb all share a common lexical origin. Therefore, to the adjectives are to be ascribed the same stem-classes which are present in nominal declension.

Since during the period when Indo-European was an ergative language, it was of the "reduced" subtype, it follows that subject/verb agreement was a comparatively late development within the language because in reduced ergative languages the verb is uninflected for person. As I proposed earlier, it was only after the adoption of a personal (first-person) marker in *-N by the verb that an inflectional opposition of personal (in *-N) : non-personal (second-third person, in *-$\emptyset$) was created. The formal identity of the *-$\emptyset$ ending of the non-personal verb and the *-$\emptyset$ termination of the noun in originally ergative function led to an interpretation of an assonance concord relationship between the two by speakers of the language and to a subsequent generalization of *-$\emptyset$ as an indicator of animate and natural agent subject in intransitive sentences. The purely formal aspects of the reanalysis would have naturally been reinforced by the intimate syntactic relationship which exists between the subject and the predicate of a sentence. Of course, this assonance concord relationship was from the beginning an imperfect one since inanimate nouns formed their nominative in *-N. When inanimate nouns appeared as subjects, the type of motion which was in operation was that attested in the dialects themselves, although it was only on analogy with the more fundamental assonance concord system that this type of motion was recognized as a viable means of denoting agreement. Thus, perhaps it was here in the subject/verb relation that the decline of the assonance concord system had much of its start. Whether or not this is true, the fact remains that assonance concord largely disappeared in the later stages of Indo-European and was replaced by what I shall term "traditional concord."

It should be emphasized that the development of assonance concord must not be construed as a simple mechanical process since it did serve an important functional role in the language. Because of the widespread appearance of motion, the stylistic benefits of greater freedom in word order were realized, for now the relation between syntactic units in a sentence was more clearly marked (Fodor 1959: 35).

The concordial relationship which existed between anaphoric pronouns and their nominal antecedents is an extremely ancient phenomenon, dating from the earliest stages of the language. From the very beginning of the period when the ergative construction characterized Indo-European syntactic structure, pronominal/nominal concord was firmly established. Indeed, the structure of the anaphoric (-demonstrative) pronoun as it is attested in the historical dialects seems to reflect the earlier ergative nature of Indo-European. Simply, it appears that a pronominal form in *so (Gk. hó, Go. sa, Skt. sá) was utilized in reference to nouns when the ergative function was to be expressed, while a form in *tod (Gk. tó, Skt. tád, Lat. is-tud, OCS to) was used when the indication of the absolute was necessary. Thus, in early Indo-European pronominal/nominal concord seems to have been manifested by means of lexically-differentiated forms (perhaps dating from the pre-inflectional stage of Indo-European when its ergative structure was characterized non-inflectionally, cf. Dixon 1979: 67 ff. regarding such ergative languages), whose occurrence depended on the case-function which was to be assumed. Even the etymologically related enclitic anaphoric pronouns of Hittite imply such lexical expression in the differences between the nominative animate -aš (whose original form was *-o) and the nominative-accusative inanimate -at, which shows the same dental as *tod.

After the ergative structure of Indo-European had been transformed into the nominative-accusative type, with a fully morphologized

category of gender, the old pronominal system naturally aligned itself with the new structural pattern. *so became interpreted as an
exponent of the nominative animate, while *tod came to mark the objective animate and the nominative-objective inanimate. Although
the concord of nouns and pronouns (which had a lexical manifesta-
tion) substantially predated the rise of assonance concord in the
adjective/noun and subject/verb relations, the pronominal system did
not remain unaffected by the prevailing tendencies of structural
evolution in the concordial system. The frequency of sentences in
which the nominal antecedent and its pronoun were utilized in an
identical function as well as the fact that such pronouns could be
employed adjectivally (as demonstratives) provided a strong motivation for them to adopt the nominal terminations. That the form *so
readily lent itself to the morphological analysis *so-∅, with an
inflectional ending *-∅ which was identical to that of the nominative of animate nouns, also encouraged this development. Because
of such influences, the pronoun *toN (Gk. tón, Skt. tám, Lat. is-tum,
OP stan) came into existence. Since the opposition animate : inanimate came to be explicitly marked in nouns and since in certain
situations the undifferentiated use of *tod in reference to animates
and inanimates alike led to semantic ambiguities, the variant form
*toN was eventually specialized as a pronoun with objective animate
value; and *tod was analyzed as a neuter form with nominative and
objective signification. The influence of assonance concord was
also probably responsible for the development of the variant *sos
(Hitt. šaš, Skt. sás) after *-s appeared as a nominative suffix in
animate nouns, although *so is generally retained in the dialects
in this function. It should be noted that the imperfect utilization
of assonance concord in pronominal reference also may have contributed to the demise of the assonance system elsewhere.

Many other factors also probably led to the widespread disappearance of the early assonance concord system and its replacement by
the traditional concord system. For example, after the introduction
of the nominative morpheme *-s into the animate declension, replacing *-∅ in most stem-classes, this same element was extended to adjectival forms. Since the same phonological constraints that limited
the distribution of *-s in the noun (see below) were also operative
in the adjective, in such cases as those involving an r-stem adjective (which retained the *-∅ marker for the same reasons as did r-
stem nouns), used to modify an animate o-stem noun (which adopted
the ending *-s), assonance concord was no longer exhibited. Other
stem-classes of nouns and adjectives also came to manifest this inherent breakdown of the early concordial system. Perhaps the next
step in this process of decline involved the invariable adoption of

the nominative animate morpheme *-*s* by the adjectives phonologically capable of adopting it when they modified any animate noun, irrespective of its termination. This development was motivated by the invariable appearance of *-*s* in the corresponding nominal stem-classes. Moreover, a similar distributional reanalysis led to the constant utilization of the nominative-objective inanimate suffix *-*N* in the *o*-stem adjectives, despite the fact that they were used to modify other neuter nouns in *-*∅*, and to the invariable utilization of the nominative-objective inanimate marker *-*∅* in adjectives not of the *o*-stem class, even when they modified *o*-stem neuter nouns in *-*N*. Parallel tendencies toward specialization of the oblique-case suffixes would have had the same results. Also, the development of a feminine form of the adjective, whose occurrence was semantically rather than formally motivated (see below), likewise contributed to the disappearance of an already dying assonance concord system. The assonance concord relation between subject and verb deteriorated as the verbal system became more and more complex and gained a greater degree of autonomy because of the highly specialized morphological categories which it came to express.

3.6.2 The Nominative Singular Animate Suffix *-*s*. Although a large number of Indo-Europeanists readily agree that the desinence *-*s* which appears in the nominative singular of various stem-classes of animate nouns is of a later origin than the *-*∅* marker of the nominative animate, the source of *-*s* has been a subject of much debate.[15] The classical view of its origin, proposed by Brugmann, Hirt, Jacobi, Biese, and Kurylowicz, is that it represents a reduction of an earlier *so*, the nominative singular animate demonstrative (anaphoric) pronoun (Lane 1951: 372), while Erhart (1967: 15) and Lehmann (1958: 188-192) believe the form to be a remnant of an earlier suffix with singularizing or individualizing function. Specht (1947: 354) seems to unite both of these assessments when he says: "Dieses *s* ist aber nichts anderes als eine deiktische Partikel, die zum Demonstrativum geworden ist." I would like to propose yet another theory about the origin of this element which crucially involves changes that took place in verbal conjugation and the existence of the assonance concord system.

As I argued earlier, the original non-personal affix in the verb was *-*∅*, which was in agreement with an animate and natural agent nominative suffix *-*∅*. However, the verb then developed a non-personal suffix *-*s* (and somewhat later a non-personal suffix *-*t*). Watkins (1962: 99), cf. Adrados 1971: 97 ff., maintains that this non-personal (for Watkins, third person) suffix *-*s* originally had no such person-indicating value: "The origin of the -*s* is to be sought in the configuration of root with final enlargement -s-." In other words, *-s was a simple root enlargement in the sense of Benveniste; i.e., it had no functional value, "it was simply a phonetic component" (Watkins 1962: 100). From this *-s enlargement, Watkins (1962: 101-102) also derives the suffix *-s- with aorist value, in addition to the desinential *-s which is of concern here. At first, the radical form in final *-s was interpreted as showing a zero ending: *preks → *preks-∅. The continued existence of the unenlarged root (*prek-) and the occurrence of a zero ending common to both resulted in a new morphological segmentation: *prek-s-∅. This *-s- was eventually assigned an aorist function. Watkins also argues that a similar process of reinterpretation was responsible for the development of the non-personal suffix *-s: "An isolated root enlarged by -s, functioning as a 3 sg. [non-personal--K.S.] with a zero ending (e.g., *dhās-∅) can be contrasted with the unenlarged root (*dhā-), which imposes a new morphemic segmentation of the 3 sg. form as *dhā-s, and the reinterpretation of the -s as a 3 sg. ending" (1962: 102).

When the *-s element was interpreted and generalized as the marker of the non-personal in verbal forms, replacing *-∅ as the primary exponent of this category, it naturally spread to those nominal forms where assonance concord was crucial in marking the subject/verb relation and became the indicator of the nominative. The so-called natural agent nouns, which by this time had lost much of their original semantic motivation, continued to preserve the *-∅ suffix, probably because of the analogical influence exerted on them by the large number of neuter nouns in *-N which did not participate in an assonance concord relationship with the verb. Moreover, this restriction on the occurrence of *-s provided a further opportunity to differentiate (i.e. hypercharacterize) the animates and the neuters. In addition, as Brugmann (1930: 346-347, 426) points out, the phonological structure of Indo-European did not permit the existence of the sequence $\bar{V}$ (= long vowel) + R (= resonant) + C (= consonant or consonantal resonant). This fact explains the exclusion of the nominative singular animate morpheme *-s from the l-, r-, m-, and n-declensions, where the nominative form adopted, for the reasons described above, a long final vowel and then analogically reintroduced the final resonant. Those variants (still attested in the historical languages) which do not show such reintroduction of the resonant did not adopt *-s as a nominative morpheme because of the influence exerted on them by their counterparts in -$\bar{V}R$.

When the element *-t became an indicator of the non-personal function in the verb, the marking of the subject/verb relation by

means of assonance concord had become largely non-productive; and
*-s and *-∅ had become crystallized as nominative markers. Thus,
there was no parallel spread of *-t into nominal declension. Perhaps the suffix *-t which appears in Sanskrit as an extension of the
neuter r-/n-stems in the nominative-accusative, e.g. *śákṛt, yákṛt*,
gen. *śaknás, yaknás*, is this same verbal suffix having been sporadically transferred to nouns as a means not so much of maintaining
assonance as of further differentiating animates (with nominatives
in *-∅ and *-s) from inanimates (with nominatives in *-∅ > *-t if
the extension had continued, and *-N).[16] However, I would not want
to make very much of this explanation of the t-suffix seen in these
nouns.

NOTES

[1] I believe that this nominative formation served to mark the vocative function as well, cf. Kurylowicz (1964: 197-199), who assumes
"an original identity of the nom. and the voc. of the sing., a nom.-
voc. with primary function = nom., secondary function = voc."

[2] The Lithuanian suffix, which also serves to mark the genitive,
has been explained in various ways. Meillet (1964: 322) argues
that it shows "intonation douce," while Endzelīns (1971: 134) says:
"The Lithuanian and the Latvian along with the OCS -a in the form
duxa '(of the) spirit' has developed from -āt < -o-at, although
originally this was an ablative ending, cf. Skt. *áśvāt* '(from the)
horse', Lat. *lupō(d)* '(from the) wolf', etc."

[3] Rosenkranz (1949) demonstrates that only Greek adverbs in -ōs
which are derived from adjectives can be considered to have an Indo-
European origin, since "die Pronominaladverbia auf -ōs seien eine
junge Bildung" (1949: 245). He also identifies the -s in this suffix with the genitive-ablative in *-(e/o)s, but denies that any
relationship exists between the formation and the ablative ending
*-ōd (1949: 246) because of his failure to recognize the autonomy
of the *-ō element.

[4] Jasanoff (1973) derives this Hittite ending from an n-stem endingless locative plus *-ti. However, since the suffix is attested
outside this declensional class, I question his analysis. The frequency with which the formation appears in n-stems is simply due to
the association of the -an- of the ending with the stem-element of
this class.

[5] *schisman* "occurs in the expression . . . : *en schisman ackewij-
stin Krixtiāniskan astin* . . . 'in this evident Christian affair'.
Endzelīns, 1944, 120, objects that elsewhere in the Old Prussian
texts there is no living locative case;" and therefore he argues
that the form "may be a misprint for *schismau* in which case the
word would be in the dative singular" (Schmalstieg 1974a: 132-133).
The nature of this form is thus subject to various interpretations.
In regard to the Indic suffix, Brugmann (1911: 181) simply observes:
". . . der Ursprung von ai. -ām unklar ist." Avestan and Old Persian show an ending in -ā (Avest. *grīvay-a* 'neck', OPers. *Arbairāy-ā*
'Arbela'), which, I feel, derives from *-oN. The Indic ending derives from a contamination of the variants *-oN and *-ō.

[6] Gray (1932: 193) says that "the origin of the long vowel in
Attic-Ionic *hēmîn, humîn*, Dor. *emín, tín, hāmín, hūmín* is rather
problematical." However, I believe that one can see here the con-

tamination of preconsonantal (*-$\bar{\imath}$) and prevocalic (*-iN) sandhi variants.

[7]Of course, the traditional analysis of the pronominal stem-formants just discussed is that they constitute reduced pronominal stems. Thus, Szemerényi (1970: 189) says of the *-sm- element: "Es ist deshalb wahrscheinlich, dass -sm- der Emphase dient, also entweder der Pronominalstamm für 'derselbe' oder eher das spätere Zahlwort *sem- 'eins' ist." The Hittite enclitic pronoun -$\check{s}ma\check{s}$ is often cited in support of this position, cf. Lane 1961: 471-472; but this is not a necessary assumption since, as Kronasser (1956: 144) suggests, the Hittite form may derive from a reduction of *e-$smas$, i.e. the pronominal stem *e-, cf. Skt. $asma\acute{\imath}$. A problem inherent in the identification of these elements as original pronouns is their occurrence only in the oblique cases. My approach naturally explains this fact. Another explanation of the origin of these formants appears in Shields 1978c: 73.

[8]Hirt (1927: 11-12) describes this particle: "Erweitert haben wir u in 1. ubi 'wo', 1. u-ti 'so', aw. $u^\cup ti$, gr. $\bar{e}$-$\acute{u}te$ 'gleichwie', ai. u-$t\acute{a}$ 'auch sogar'. Aus dem Gegensatz von i-bi und u-bi ergibt sich wohl die Bedeutung 'hier' und 'da' für i und u." Since this particle appears only in the locative(-genitive) and in an accessory capacity at that, I feel that it is not really a desinence, but is simply an adverb. Although all the oblique case markers probably had the same adverbial origin, they became true inflectional elements. The suffix *-u which appears in the dual nominative-accusative is not etymologically related to this adverbial particle; instead, it "could well come from the numeral for 'two', cf. Skt. $d(u)v\bar{a}u$, Armenian $erku$, Lat. duo, Old Irish dau, do, and da, Welsh dou, etc." (Schmalstieg 1974c: 189).

[9]Since there exists a plural morpheme *-s, whose origin is obviously rather late in the development of Indo-European, it is impossible to determine precisely whether it is this element or the oblique case marker *-s which appears in the plural case-forms of the various oblique cases. Thus, for example, Kuryłowicz (1964: 201) says of the Sanskrit instrumental plural suffix -$bhis$ and the dative-ablative plural suffix -$bhyas$: "Whether the s of *-$bhis$ is to be regarded as the sign of the plur. and the -os of *-$bhios$ as a reinforcement designed to stress the abl. function (-os =^ending of the gen.-abl. sing.) cannot be decided for certain." However, I believe that the identification of this *-s of the locative plural as the oblique suffix has validity since it does occur in the locative dual as well.

[10]As Poultney (1967: 872) observes: "The situation in Greek is complicated and not wholly clear. Epic $to\hat{\imath}o$ 'his', $theo\hat{\imath}o$ 'god's', etc. give abundant evidence of -syo (-oio < *-$osyo$); but Epic -ou, -oo (split between feet and scanned $\cup$_ before CC . . .), Att.-Ion. -ou are ambiguous: either -ou is from -oo < *-oso, or -ou is from -oo < -oio < *-$osyo$."

[11]A useful summary of the more important theories concerning the origin of -$\bar{e}$ appears in Lehmann 1967: 108-109. The most recent proposal is presented in Bech 1969.

[12]As Buck (1933: 181) points out: "The L. -$\bar{\imath}$, which is an inherited -$\bar{\imath}$, as shown by the uniform spelling in the early inscriptions in which there is no confusion of $\bar{\imath}$ and ei, has no connection with . . . [IE *-o-$s\r{\imath}o$--K.S.]." A very clear and concise presentation of the major theories concerning the origin of the Italic and Celtic genitive singular in -$\bar{\imath}$ appears in Coleman 1972. Although Coleman shows that certain theories seem more credible than others, he concludes that no one hypothesis is definitive and calls for scholars "to extend the discussion [of the origin of the ending--K.S.] beyond the confines set by the previous literature," since only through "carefully controlled" "speculative ventures . . . are we likely to

achieve any progress on the thematic genitive singular" (1972: 78).
In a recent important article, Watkins (1967: 38) writes in regard
to the desinence $-\bar{\imath}$, cf. Brugmann 1911: 121-122: "I find it hard to
separate the 'feminine' $-\bar{\imath}$." Howevever, this view is strongly attacked by Dyen (1974: 135). In short, it seems that the origin of
the Italo-Celtic suffix remains an enigma.

[13] In other words, I do not believe that the $-t-$ of the Tocharian
suffix is an epenthetic sound, cf. Krause and Thomas 1960: 104. I
should point out that the origin of the dental suffix in the ablative and the instrumental forms which I have cited has been a subject of much debate. Sturtevant (1932: 3-4) sees it as a sandhi
variant of $*-ts$, a position strongly attacked by Erhart (1970: 118)
and Kronasser (1956: 101-102). Kurylowicz (1964: 194) identifies
it as the "union consonant," while Meillet (1964: 322) says that it
is "une postposition $-d$ $(-t)$ indiquant le point de départ, cf. lat.
$d\bar{e}$." Specht (1947: 365) believes the ending to be an original demonstrative stem in $*t/d-$, and Burrow (1973: 279) suggests that it
represents a reanalyzed stem-final element of the t-stems. Erhart
(1970: 131) sees it as an original elative case-marker, and Adrados
(1975: 453), as an ablative "alargamiento" with secondary instrumental function and with a possible etymological relationship to
the neuter pronominal suffix $*-d$ (cf. Skt. $t\acute{a}d$). Elsewhere (1978b:
206-207) I have argued that it is an old nominative marker; but I
now prefer Szemerényi's identification (1956: 68) of $*-T$ as an original adverbial element.

[14] It is interesting to note that despite the specialization and
subsequent generalization of the ablative suffix $-(a)z$ in Hittite,
resulting in the separation of the genitive and the ablative in all
stem-classes, Sturtevant (1933: 166) emphasizes that the substitution of a genitive for an expected ablative does occur, this perhaps
being a relic of their original formal identity. Of course, the
limited generalization of the o-stem suffix of Indo-European proper
$(*-\bar{e}/\bar{o}T)$ takes place in some dialects. As Burrow (1973: 233) says:
"In certain languages, notably in Italic and the later Avestan, this
form is extended to other classes (Osc. $toutad$ 'civitate', Lat.
$magistratud$, Av. $\bar{a}\theta rat$, $garoit$, etc.)."

[15] At the time of the introduction of this morpheme, the singular
number was beginning to be distinguished from the non-singular,
which was characterized by the markers $*-N$ and $*-i$. Therefore, it
is assumed that the element $*-s$ was generally specialized in the
singular not long after it became a productive suffix in the inflectional system.

[16] The etymological connection between the $-t$ seen in these Sanskrit
nominative-accusative neuter forms and the $-t-$ found in the oblique
cases of the Greek $r-/n-$stems, e.g. Gk. gen. sg. $o\acute{u}thatos$ (cf. Skt.
$\bar{u}dhnas$) 'udder', and in the Greek neuter n-stems generally, e.g. Gk.
gen. sg. $on\acute{o}mata$ (cf. Skt. $n\acute{a}mnas$) 'name', is a complicated issue
that I feel is not worth pursuing here. It may be that the Greek
forms attest the old oblique marker $*-T$, not the extended verbal ending $*-t$, although the occurrence of the Sanskrit suffix and the Greek
suffix in the same stem-class seems to speak for their common origin.
In the final analysis, "The precise source of the Greek t-inflection
is uncertain" (Buck 1933: 189).

4 The Origin of the Non-Singular and the Development of the Feminine Gender

4.   In this chapter I intend to discuss the appearance of the
non-singular (dual-plural) inflectional category and to relate its
origin to the development of the feminine gender. As I have indicated before, I believe that the appearance of specifically non-
singular constructions was rather late in the evolution of the Indo-
European language. But in the course of time, three inflectional
suffixes came to express non-singularity—*-N, *-i, and, perhaps
somewhat later, *-s. The fact that *-N and *-i are attested in both
the dual and the plural suggests the original unity of these two
numbers in a single category. Schmalstieg (1974c: 192) thus says:
"Evidence for the assumption that dual and plural were not clearly
distinguished at an early period of Indo-European comes from the
fact that the *ā-stem ending *-ai functions as a plural marker in
Greek and Latin (cf. Gk. khôr-ai 'lands', Lat. port-ae 'doors'),
whereas in Sanskrit and Balto-Slavic the same ending marks the dual
(cf. Skt. bāl-e '(two) maidens', OCS rǫc-ě, Lith. rank-ì [< *-ai]
'(two) hands'). Likewise the *o-stem ending *-oi furnishes nominative plurals for masculine nouns in Balto-Slavic (cf. OCS grad-i
'cities', Lith. výr-ai 'men [< *-oi]), but duals for neuters in
Slavic and Sanskrit (cf. OCS měst-ě '(two) places', Skt. phal-e
'(two) fruits')." Although *-s is limited to plural function in the
historical dialects, the occurrence of *-N and *-i as well in plural
function implies that no significant differences in denotation among
the three suffixes originally existed. That is, in Indo-European
they apparently represented a classic instance of paradigmatic polymorphy. Still, it is possible that these three elements "may have
had various kinds of non-singular meanings which we can no longer
distinguish" (Schmalstieg 1980: 74); but I shall not speculate
about this matter. (See Schmalstieg 1980: 73-75 in regard to some
possibilities.) Nevertheless, I would suggest that as part of their
general function of indicating non-singularity, at least one or two
of these desinences could be used as a collective marker. To be
sure, the secondary use of non-singular markers in collective func-

tion is widely attested in the Indo-European languages (Kurylowicz
1964: 204). In fact, the original function of these suffixes may
perhaps have been exclusively collective signification, if Kurylowicz' observation (1964: 204) that in the historical development
of natural languages, the plural (non-singular) "is at the same time
the result of the *grammaticalization* of the collective" can be accepted as correct. It is interesting to note that these non-singular suffixes are homophonous with the oblique inflections *-N*, *-i*,
and *-s*; but I leave open the question of their etymological relationship. As Schmalstieg (1977b: 145) says, "The elements *-N*,
-i, and *-s* may or may not have had an original etymological connection with the same phonemes when they functioned as case markers
in the noun. Thus, for example, one can compare the usage of the
English morpheme *-s* which functions with both a plural and a genitive meaning, but for the average speaker of English there is no
common semantic bond between the two functions."

4.1   The Non-Singular Markers. Since Schmalstieg (1977b: 129-144;
1980: 73-87) has provided detailed descriptions of the occurrence
of the non-singular endings *-N*, *-i*, and *-s* in the historical dialects, I shall, in general, only briefly point out some attested
suffixes in which they appear. However, the importance of the marker
-N in the evolution of the feminine gender, the fact that its existence is somewhat less certain than the other two suffixes', and some
additional conclusions that I have reached concerning its development which are not presented in Schmalstieg's discussions require
that I devote substantially more attention to *-N*.

4.1.1 The Non-Singular Marker *-N*. The use of a nasal as an indicator of the non-singular is attested in a number of the Indo-European dialects. In Tocharian, for example, there exists a nominative
plural ending in -*ñ*: AB *riñ* 'cities', A *yukañ* 'horses', A *pyāpyāñ*,
B *pyapyaiñ* 'flowers', cf. Schmalstieg 1980: 75.[1] Moreover, in
Tocharian A nominative-oblique dual ("Paral," cf. Krause and Thomas
1960: 76-77) nouns end in -($\ddot{a}$)*ṃ*, while Tocharian B generally shows
-(*a*)*ne* as a marker of this nominal function.
    It has been suggested that the nasal in certain Sanskrit *o-*, *i-*,
and *u*-stem nominative-accusative neuter plural forms, such as
bhúvanāni (which alternates with *bhúvanā* in the Vedic language,
but which is generalized in later Sanskrit) 'worlds', *śúcīni* (which
similarly alternates with *śúcī*) 'bright ones', and *vásūni* (which
similarly alternates with *vásū*) 'possessions', has been analogically
introduced from the *n-* and *nt*-stems. However, I maintain that the
termination -$\bar{V}ni$ which is attested in all of these forms is a result

of the passage of *-*VN* to *-*V̄*, with the analogical reintroduction
of the non-singular marker *-*N*, motivated by the simple contamination of sandhi variants (one in *-*V̄* and the other in *-*VN*). The
somewhat later affixed -*i* is simply another marker of the non-singular. Iranian also shows traces of this formation, but without the
-*i*: "Im Av. auch -*ąn* (-*ąm* -*ą*): *amašyąn* -*yą* (*amašya*- 'menschenleer'),
gthav. *vīspə̄ng* (*vīspa*- 'all'), *yąm* (Pronom. *ya*-). . . . Im Av.
könnte man *-*īn*, *-*ūn* als Parallele zu *-*ān* erwarten, und da das Av.
die nasalierten *i*- und *u*-Vokale in der Schrift nicht besonders be-
zeichnete, so ist möglich, dass die Schreibungen -*ĭ̃*, -*ŭ̃* zugleich -*ị̄*,
-*ụ̄* meinten" (Brugmann 1911: 233-234). I would also suggest that
certain corresponding *i*- and *u*-stem duals of these Sanskrit forms
show the non-singular formations *-*iN* and *-*uN*, along with the final
suffix *-*i*, lengthened because of the influence exerted by the numerous dual constructions in a final long vowel: *śúcinī* 'two bright
ones', *vásunī* 'two possessions'.

I believe, cf. Schmalstieg 1977b: 131, that the plural suffix
*-*nt*-, found in both Tocharian (A -*nt*, -*ntu*; B -*nta*) and Luwian
(-*nzi* [nom.], -*nza* [acc.-dat]) also shows this same non-singular
nasal suffix in contamination with an element *-*t* (which, according
to Schmalstieg 1977b: 131-132, may also have had some kind of non-
singular value). "In Hittite, Indo-Iranian, Slavic and perhaps in
Greek we find -*nt*- more or less clearly as a collective suffix according to Erhart [(1970: 79)--K.S.]. Sturtevant, 1951: 79 cites
such forms as *an-tu-uḫ-ša-an-na-an-za* 'people' as opposed to *an-tu-*
uḫ-ša-aš 'man'; *ud-ne-ya-an-za, ud-ni-ya-an-za, ud-ne-e-an-za*, acc.
ud-ni-an-da-an 'population' as opposed to *ud-ne(-e), ud-ni-e,*
ud-ni-i 'country'" (Schmalstieg 1977b: 131). Perrot (1961: 335-
340) argues that the collective desinence *-*nt*- is also attested in
Latin, specifically in the suffix -*mentum*, although its original
collective value is largely obscured. He proposes that -*mentum* derives from an old collective formation which has been thematicized
and reinterpreted as "un singulatif" (1961: 340) and further maintains that this old collective suffix *-*m-n̥t*- was frequently hyper-
characterized by the collective marker *-*ā̄/-ə*, as the neuter plural
desinence -*menta* demonstrates (1961: 338-339).

I also feel that the non-consonant-stem animate nouns, with an
original *-*∅* case ending in the nominative, formed a generalized (in
terms of case functions) non-singular variant by adding to the stem
the suffix *-*N*: *-*o-N*, *-*a-N*, *-*i-N*, and *-*u-N*. Because of phonological changes (the monophthongization of *-*VN* in preconsonantal
position), the following pairs of sandhi doublets were created:
*-*oN/*-*ō*, *-*aN/*-*ā*, *-*iN/*-*ī*, and *-*uN/*-*ū*. Only the preconsonantal forms are generally retained in the non-singular function in the

historical dialects, where they are attested as markers of the nominative-accusative dual (Schmalstieg 1977b: 132-133): *-ō: Skt.
vŕ̥kā, Avest. vǝhrka, Gk. lúkō, OCS vlъka 'two wolves'; *-ī: Skt. ávī
'two sheep', Lith. naktì, OCS nošti 'two nights'; *-ū: Skt. sū́nū,
Lith. sū́nu, OCS syny 'two sons', Avest. bāzu 'two arms'. Perhaps
Tocharian shows a contamination of the two stem-variants in the
dual (paral) form A pärwāṃ (B pärwāne) 'eyebrows', whose -ā- Petersen (1939: 95-96) compares to the dual suffix of Skt. bhrúvā (sg.
bhrū́s 'eyebrow'). Since the a-stems were later assimilated into the
ā-stems, the original situation in this class remains obscured. Interestingly enough, Greek does point to the existence of a nominative-accusative dual ending in *-ā in a few ā-stem nouns, e.g.
khṓrā 'two lands', númphā 'two nymphs', reflecting perhaps the parallel development of *-aN to *-ā, although these forms may simply represent analogical reformulations based on stems in *-o. The traditional reconstruction of the ā-stem dual in Balto-Slavic and Indo-
Iranian, and the ā-stem plural in Greek and Latin, *-ai, may also
perhaps represent this suffix *-ā in contamination with the non-
singular marker *-i.

That these suffixes initially served as generalized non-singular
markers is demonstrated by the identity of the nominative and the
accusative in the dual of the various historical dialects, the category which frequently reflects the structure of the original non-
singular formations in Indo-European. The rather late origin of
other case distinctions of the dual is indicated by the wide variety
of formations which are attested. Indeed, "The Hittite relic form
of the dual, šakuwa 'eyes', functions in the most ancient texts not
only as nominative and accusative, but also as dative. This should
be compared with the fact that in other Indo-European languages the
oblique cases of the dual originated in the period of dialectal development on the basis of the form later functioning as nominative
(e.g. ancient Indian dvā : dvā-bhyām, Latin duō : duō-bus, etc.)"
(Kurylowicz 1958: 250).[2]

At a somewhat later date, the non-singular suffix *-s was added
to these endings (*-ō, *-ī, *-ū), yielding *-ōs, *-īs, and *-ūs,
which became nominative-accusative plural forms (Schmalstieg 1974c:
192). The contamination of the long-vowel suffixes with *-s brought
about the specialization of *-ō, *-ī, and *-ū to dual function.
"New nominative plural forms and new accusative plural forms moved
in to cause the old generalized nom.-acc. pl. to become specialized
either in the nominative function or the accusative function. For
the *o-stem masculine [= animate--K.S.] nouns, the form with the
marker *-i became specialized as the new nominative plural, cf. Gk.
ánthrōp-oi 'men', OCS grad-i 'cities' (< *-oi), Lat. lup-ī 'wolves'

(< *-oi). This ending forced the old generalized nom.-acc. ending
*-ōs either to adopt the accusative plural function or else to be
lost completely in case the new accusative plural was encroaching
on the territory of the *-ōs acc. pl. The new accusative plural was
formed by the addition of *-s to the old accusative singular and for
the *o-stem nouns assumed the form *-oNs . . . " (Schmalstieg 1974b:
5-6). Through similar evolutionary processes, the other major stem-
classes likewise underwent an increase in the number of specialized
non-singular case-markers. (See Schmalstieg 1980: 78-87 in this
regard.)

In the inanimate nouns, a parallel sequence of events occurred.
At the time when the non-singular morpheme *-N was added to nouns,
I believe that the neuter substantives had essentially assumed the
characteristic features which they are seen to possess in the historical dialects. That is, only the o-stem nouns generally manifested the nominative-accusative (< objective) marker *-N. Of
course, with the assimilation of the a-stems and the new ā-class,
the originally neuter nouns in *-a became feminines.[3] Thus, the
nominative-accusative endings of the various neuter declensions relevant to the discussion were as follows: o-stem, *-o-N; i-stem,
*-i-∅; a-stem, *-a-∅; and u-stem, *-u-∅. Apparently the non-singu-
lar morpheme *-N came to be affixed only to those forms with the
*-∅ ending, i.e. to the stem. Through monophthongization, certain
sandhi doublets were created: *-iN/*-ī, *-aN/*-ā, and *-uN/*-ū.
The suffix *-ī is attested as a marker of the nominative-accusative
dual of the neuter i-stems (Skt. akṣī́, Avest. aši, OCS oči, Lith.
akì 'two eyes') as well as the nominative-accusative plural of this
class (Skt. trī́, OCS tri, OIr. trī 'three', Lat. trī(-gintā)
'thirty'), while *-ū serves as a nominative-accusative plural marker
in the neuter u-stems (Skt. mádhū 'honeys'). *-ī has come to be
generalized as the marker of the nominative-accusative dual in the
u-stem class (Skt. mádhvī 'two honeys'). Of course, these lengthened-
vowel suffixes served as simple non-singular constructions in early
Indo-European. It is interesting to note that the historical distribution of *-ī in the neuter i-stems clearly demonstrates its original undifferentiated dual-plural role.

Whether or not the non-singular marker *-N appeared in the neuter
o-stems cannot be definitively ascertained since it seems that the
a-stem suffix *-ā has been generalized here in the plural (Skt.
yugā́, Lat. juga, Go. juka, OCS iga 'yokes') and that a suffix in
*-oi has come to mark the dual (Skt. yugé, OCS idzě 'two yokes').
However, it is possible that not only the o-stem nominative-accusative neuter plural ending *-ā but also the o-stem nominative-accusative dual ending reflects the a-stem non-singular suffix since

the dual desinence can be reconstructed as *-ai (< *-$\bar{a}i$), cf. Gray
1932: 197, a contamination of the a-stem ending (*-$\bar{a}$) and the non-
singular morpheme *-i. In any case, I would like to suggest that
the non-singular suffix *-N was never directly added to neuter
o-stem forms. Only after the passage of *-aN to *-$\bar{a}$ did the neuter
o-stems acquire a productive non-singular ending. This conclusion
is reinforced by the fact that there is no evidence to indicate that
the non-singular marker *-N was generally affixed to consonant stem
nouns, neuter or animate. In the case of the neuter consonant stems,
it seems that the suffix *-$\bar{a}$ became generalized to a large degree
(perhaps by way of the o-stems) in the plural of certain dialects
(Go. *namna*, OCS *jimena* 'names', *slovesa* 'words', Lat. *trigintā*
'thirty', *corda* 'hearts', *nōmina* 'names'), although other non-singular formations do exist. However, none of these suggests the Indo-
European utilization of *-N. The fact that a number of undifferentiated singular/non-singular neuter consonant stem nouns in the
nominative-accusative function are retained in Vedic Sanskrit, Homeric Greek, and perhaps Hittite implies the relative modernity of
the widespread adoption of special non-singular endings by this
group, cf. Hom. *hêmar* 'day(s)'. The animate consonant stems have
also generalized a vocalic-stem termination in the attested dual
function—that of the o-stems (Skt. *pitárā* 'two fathers', *śvā́nā* 'two
dogs', Avest. *mātara* 'two mothers'); yet, once again, other constructions unrelated to the nasal suffix are found, e.g. Gk. *mētére* 'two
mothers'. Thus, it seems that the general rule for the formation of
non-singular nouns by means of the suffix *-N was simply: affix
*-N to the nominative form, if that form is terminated in a vowel or
a vocalic resonant. Although the basis for such limitation is not
immediately clear, any nominative noun with the phonological structure -$C\#$ apparently could not utilize the morpheme *-N in the formation of the non-singular. Only by analogical extension and the use
of other non-singular markers was the asymmetry in the distribution
of non-singular constructions overcome. The fact that the occurrence
of *-N was determined by the phonological structure of a case-bear-
ing form perhaps suggests that *-N was originally an enclitic adverb
of some sort. Indeed, I see this as a plausible source for all of
the non-singular markers of Indo-European, cf. Schmalstieg 1974b: 1.

I would like to suggest further that the non-singular ending *-$\bar{a}$
of the animate a-stems also sporadically spread to the animate o-
stems, perhaps on analogy with developments in the inanimate class.
The archaic remains of this extension can be seen in the so-called
"nouns of variable gender": Lat. *locus* 'place', *locī* 'places', *loca*
'region'; Lat. *jocus* 'joke', *jocī* 'jokes', *joca* 'jokes'; Gk. *sîtos*
'wheat, corn', *sîta* 'wheat, corn'; Gk. *desmós* 'string', *desmoí*

'strings', *desmá* 'strings' (Buck 1933: 207). In a number of cases,
two plural forms continue to exist side by side, each having assumed
a special meaning. Although it is traditionally argued that the
forms in *-ā̆* directly "reflect an association between the neuter
plural and a collective," with a general collective marker *-ā̆* (>
neuter plural) being used here in animate nouns, the observation
made by Buck (1933: 207) that only some of these animate nouns terminated in *-ā̆* possess any hint of a collective value and the arguments already presented on the origin of *-ā̆* suggest the validity of
the explanation just offered. Those instances where *-ā̆* assumed the
collective function are readily interpreted as natural consequences
of one of the variant forms being assigned the primary function of
the formation (plural) and the other, the secondary (collective).
Apparently *-ā̆* was specialized in the secondary function in a number
of important cases, leading to its frequent generalization in this
capacity in this substantive-type. Because of the rarity of *-ā̆* as
a non-singular marker in the animate *o*-stems and the subsequent generalization of *-ā̆* in the neuter *o*-stems, such animate forms with
the ending *-ā̆* were later interpreted as neuters.

It should be noted in passing that the secondary collective use
of the non-singular markers tended to be distinguished from the primary non-singular function not only by a difference of meaning but
also by rules of concord. That is, with a collective subject, the
verb at times assumed a singular ending. This usage is still attested with great regularity in Greek in the case of the neuter plural used in a collective sense, although this language seems in many
instances to have generalized such agreement beyond the collective
function. This usage is also sporadically retained under the same
circumstances in Sanskrit and Hittite. Thus, Kurylowicz (1964: 206)
observes: "The finite verb depending on a neuter plur. is used in
the plur. or in the sing. depending on the (primary or secondary)
function of the plur." This development is a result of what Jespersen (1935: 196) calls "the double-sidedness of collectives"; that
is, "They are units, and as such can be used not only with *a* or *one*
preposed, but also in the plural in the same way as other countables
. . . . On the other hand, they denote plurality, and therefore may
take the verb and the predicative in the plural. . . ."

Obviously, as the immediately preceding remarks imply, the singu-
lar/non-singular distinction was extended to the verb in later Indo-
European; and the marker *-N* is also used there as an indicator of
non-singularity: e.g. 3rd pl.: Skt. *-anti*, *-anta*, *-ran*, Avest.
-ənti, Gk. *-onto*, Lat. *-unt*, Go. *-and*, OCS *-ǫtъ*, Hitt. *-anzi*; 2nd
du.: Skt. *-tam*, Avest. *-təm*, Gk. *-ton*; 3rd du.: Skt. *-tām*, Gk.
-tēn. The preconsonantal variant of the verbal suffix in *-oN* is

perhaps seen in the imperative suffix *-tōt (< *-toN + *-t), cf.
Skt. -tāt, Gk. -tō, Lat. -tō < OLat. -tōd (Shields 1978a). Indeed,
Schmalstieg (1974c: 190) argues that the original form of the Indo-
European third person plural ending was *-(e/o)N and that this suffix is still attested in the dialects: "The Greek 3rd pl. active
imperfect épher-on is usually considered cognate with the Sanskrit
3rd pl. active imperfect ábhar-an. It is usually assumed that in
these forms a final *-t has been lost both in Greek and Sanskrit,
but the assumption is unnecessary. Both forms could reflect final
*-oN, i.e. the thematic vowel plus the plural marker *-N. Likewise,
it is usually thought that the OCS 3rd pl. aorist ending encountered
in (id-)ǫ '(they) went' reflects Indo-European *-ont. Again the
assumption of a final *-t is unnecessary. An Indo-European final
*-oN would have passed to Proto-Slavic *-uN which could have devel-
oped either into *-ŭ > -ъ or -y̨ = -ǫ. In this case the latter variant was chosen. . . . Similarly, the Gothic 3rd pl. secondary ending
-un may reflect IE *-y̨ without a final *-t." This same suffix *-oN
is also perhaps attested without final *-t in the Lithuanian nominative plural present active participle in -ǫ, "if this is an etymological 3rd pl. as Cowgill, 1970, suggests" (Schmalstieg 1976b: 25),
in Tocharian B 3rd pl. paḷk-eṃ (pälken-ne) and other verbs of this
type (Schmalstieg 1977a), and in the problematic Oscan-Umbrian 3rd
pl. sec. -ns (< *-N + -is, cf. Lat. -is-tī) (Shields 1980c).

4.1.2 The Non-Singular Markers *-i and *-s. I have already indicated a number of endings which show the non-singular suffixes *-i
and *-s within the context of my discussion of *-N, but I shall
briefly reiterate several examples here. In regard to the former
suffix, Schmalstieg (1980: 84) says: "The ending -y added to the
*o-stem gives the pronominal non-singular ending *-oy, and the end-
ing which is attested in such nom. pl. masc. forms as Lat. (lup-)ī
. . . , Lith. (vilk-)aĩ, Greek (lúk-)oi, OCS (vlьc-)i 'wolves'.
The same ending undoubtedly functions as a nom.-acc. *o-stem dual
in Skt. (yug-)e, OCS (i(d)z-)ě 'two yokes'." Likewise, Burrow
(1973: 237) argues: "A neuter plural suffix -i is found in Hittite
(kururi pl. of kurur nt. 'hostility'), which testifies to its antiquity in Indo-European as a method of forming the neuter plural,"
cf. Skt. nā́māni 'names'. Of course, "An s appears in most of the
plural cases, e.g. [Skt.--K.S.] acc. -ns, instr. -bhis, dat. abl.
-bhyas . . ." (Burrow 1973: 235-236). In the nominative and the
accusative masculine (= animate), this suffix frequently became
contaminated with the non-singular formations in *-ō, *-ī, and *ū,
cf., e.g. Go. nom. pl. dagōs 'days', Skt. nom. pl. dēvā́s 'gods',

Lat. acc. pl. *lupōs*, Lith. acc. pl. *vilkùs* 'wolves' (Schmalstieg
1980: 79-80). Apparently *-s* was eventually limited to plural (vs.
dual) expression.

4.2 The Neuter Plural of Consonant Stems.

Before proceeding to
my discussion of the origin of the feminine gender, I would like to
demonstrate further the utility and the versatility of the analysis
of the development of the category of number which I have just presented by commenting on certain neuter plural formations of the
consonant stem nouns.

In Iranian there exists a series of nominative-accusative neuter
plurals in the consonant stems characterized by vṛddhi of the suffix,
e.g. Avest. *ayārē* 'days', *vačā* 'words', *nāman* 'names'. The fact
that this construction is an ancient one is suggested by a few similar examples in Germanic (Go. *fidwōr* 'four', *hairtōna* 'hearts',
augōna 'eyes')[4] and Italic (Lat. *quattuor* 'four', *ōciōra* 'swifter').
In Greek such neuter forms with a lengthtned grade vowel appear as
singulars: *húdōr* 'water', *tékmōr* 'end, boundary, sign'. However,
Burrow (1973: 237) argues that "these may be old plural forms utilized as singulars after the type had died out as a plural formation." Classical Sanskrit shows neuter plurals of this type extended
by the non-singular suffix *-i*: *nāmāni* 'names'. The Vedic language,
nevertheless, still retains the ancient structure in the neuter
n-stems: *bhúmā* 'beings', *áhā* 'days', *śīrṣā* 'heads'. I would suggest that these nouns and others like them preserve the results of
the monophthongization of $V + l$, r, m, $n > \bar{V}$ in preconsonantal sandhi
position. Of course, as is evidenced in several cases here, contamination of the two sandhi doublets often led to the analogical
reintroduction of the final resonant. Moreover, it appears that
such vocalic lengthening was analogically extended as a morphological marker to certain other consonant stem classes, as the following
s-stem forms demonstrate: Avest. *manā*, Skt. *mánąsi* 'thoughts,
minds', *durmanąsi* 'troubled ones'.[5] The new long-vowel forms, derived from an original undifferentiated nominative-accusative singu-
lar/non-singular construction, were analyzed as non-singulars,
probably on analogy with non-singular nouns terminated in a long
vowel (derived from $*-V-N$ [= non-singular $*-N$]).

It is important to recall that in the consonant stems of the animate declension, the nominative (> nominative singular) came to be
differentiated from corresponding vocative by such vocalic lengthening, cf. Gk. nom. sg. *mḗtēr* 'mother', voc. sg. *mḗter* 'O, mother'.
Obviously the long-vowel forms of both the animate and the inanimate
classes result from the same phonological changes. However, in the

neuter class the specialization of sandhi variants proceeded differently because the need for neuter vocatives was minimal.

Neuter plurals made by suffixing the element *-i to such vr̥ddhied
forms appear not only in Sanskrit but also in Avestan as alternates
to the simple long-vowel plurals: $n\bar{a}m\bar{ə}ni$ 'names', $s\bar{a}x^v\bar{ə}n\bar{\imath}$ (< *-i)
'teachings', $varə\check{c}\bar{a}h\bar{\imath}$ (< *-i) 'energies'. This -i, which hyperchar-
acterizes these forms, is generally derived from Indo-European *-$ə$.
However, the existence of a parallel neuter plural in -i in Hittite
($kururi$ 'hostilities') and the occurrence of *-i in the dual of the
neuter consonant stems (although this suffix has largely been
lengthened under the influence of the dual endings of many other
stem-classes), cf. Skt. $j\acute{a}nas$-$\bar{\imath}$ 'two races', $n\acute{a}man$-$\bar{\imath}$ 'two names',
Lat. ($v\bar{\imath}$-)$gint$-$\bar{\imath}$ 'twenty', OCS $sloves$-i 'two words', $jimen$-i 'two
names', Att. ($e\acute{\imath}$-)kos-i 'twenty' (with short *-i), Boeot. ($p\acute{\imath}$-)kat-i
'twenty' (with short *-i), lead me to believe that the -i is origin-
al here. Moreover, the validity of the identification of IE *$ə$ and
II i has recently come into question.[6] Thus, the suffix -i in the
neuter plural of Indo-Iranian consonant stem nouns seems to be the
non-singular indicator *-i, cf. Burrow 1973: 237-238.

Certain Indo-European languages seem to attest the generalization
of the vocalic stem ending *-$\bar{a}$ in the plural function in a number of
neuter consonant stem classes, while others appear to show the reduced grade of this suffix in these same environments. It is frequently rather difficult to determine which form of the suffix is
present in the various nouns because of the ambiguity of orthographic
evidence. Brugmann (1904: 393) argues that Italic (Lat. $n\bar{o}mina$
'names'), Germanic (Go. $hairt\bar{o}na$ 'hearts', $namna$ 'names'), and
Slavic (OCS $jimena$ 'names') show original consonant stem plurals in
*-$\bar{a}$ rather than *-$ə$. On the other hand, he maintains that Greek
attests *-$ə$ in the neuter plural function ($on\acute{o}mata$ 'names'), with
the reduced grade of the suffix appearing also in the vocalic stems
($dzug\acute{a}$ 'yokes', $g\acute{e}nea$ 'races, kinds'). However, I would suggest,
given the tenuous position of IE *$ə$, that the Greek ending may derive from the specifically Greek use of the non-singular suffix *-N
in the consonant stems (*-$\underset{\circ}{N}$ > -a), with this ending being extended
to the vocalic declensions. The apparent limitation of this construction to Greek precludes assigning the suffix *-N to the consonant stems in Indo-European.

4.3   The Origin of the Feminine Gender. As Schmidt (1889) demonstrates, the close relationship (in terms of formal identity and
syntactic patterning) which exists between the primary feminine
markers *-$\bar{a}$, *-$\bar{\imath}$, and *-$\bar{u}$ and certain neuter plural endings makes it
necessary to consider both simultaneously in an investigation of the

sources of the feminine gender. Indeed, he argues that the characteristic suffixes of the feminine gender originally had nothing to
do with the indication of the feminine gender category. Rather,
after studying the various methods of forming nominative-accusative
plural neuters in the Indo-European dialects, he discovered that
"none of them were distinct from methods of forming nominative singular feminines, and concluded that in Proto-Indo-European neuter
plurals were actually singular collectives" (Lehmann 1958: 179).
Thus, on the basis of Schmidt's work, it has traditionally come to
be held that the original function of these feminine suffixes was
the formation of collectives and abstracts, cf. Brugmann 1911: 231-
232. As Conway (1889: 469) notes, the collective and the abstract
functions are closely related semantically, with the former giving
rise to the latter through a simple process of semantic generalization. However, I believe that Schmidt's view is far too narrow in
terms of just what phenomena are to be connected in a general explanation of the origin of the feminine gender.

Basing his hypothesis on Schmidt's ideas, Brugmann (1897) attempts
to explain the developmental relationship among collectives, abstracts, and the feminine gender. Since forms with abstract signification can be used in reference to concrete concepts, such terms
expressing an abstract quality often "come to be used to denote the
individual person or thing which possesses that quality" (Brugmann
1897: 26). Moreover, terms of collective signification can come to
be employed to designate individuals (Brugmann 1897: 26). Brugmann
(1897: 26-27) observes that such developments are not infrequent in
the evolution of the historical Indo-European languages; forms which
have been affected by these processes include the English words *youth*
and *beauty*, and the German words *Schönheit* 'beauty', *Bedienung* 'service',
Aufwartung 'attendance', and *Frauenzimmer* 'woman'. Thus, the Indo-European etyma of Lat. *nauta* 'sailor', which probably meant 'sailoring' or
the like originally, and Lat. *aurīga* 'charioteer', which probably
had the sense 'driving' originally, lost their abstract signification and became concrete in reference. Brugmann (1897: 27) argues
that one or more words of this abstract and collective group, coming
into concrete value by a change of meaning like that just described,
happened to denote an object with natural female sex. In the class
of $\bar{a}$-stem nouns, he suggests that $*g^w en\bar{a}$ 'woman' (Skt. $gn\acute{\bar{a}}$ [< $*g^w n\bar{a}$],
Gk. $gun\acute{e}$, OIr. *ben*, Go. *qinō*, OCS *žena*), for example, was originally
an abstract or a collective meaning 'bearing', or 'parturition'.
The word then changed its denotation to the more concrete 'animal
that bears' and then 'woman'. In this noun and probably a number of
similar ones, e.g. $*m\bar{a}$ (with reduplicated variants $*m\breve{a}m\bar{a}$, $*mamm\bar{a}$)
'mother' (Skt. $m\acute{\bar{a}}$, Att. *mámmē*, Lat. *mamma*, Lith. *mamà*), $*-\bar{a}$ became

morphologically segmented, or morphologically reanalyzed, as a marker
of female sex (Brugmann 1897: 27-30). That is, the semantic feature (Female) was given formal expression because one or more forms
possessing this feature also had the formal property which came to
serve as its exponent. Similarly, "The $-\bar{\imath}$ ending in the $-\bar{\imath}$-, $-\underset{\frown}{\imath}\bar{a}$-
declension came to be abstracted as a female suffix on account of
the meaning of $*str\bar{\imath}$ 'woman'" (Fodor 1959: 16).[7] The value of $*-\bar{u}$
was derived by an identical process. Perhaps the common functions
served by $*-\bar{a}$, $*-\bar{\imath}$, and $*-\bar{u}$ in forming abstracts and collectives
also led to some mutual influences in their specialization in this
further morphological use. The validity of Brugmann's analysis is
strongly implied by a recent study done by Miranda (1975), in which
he shows that a similar sequence of events has occurred in Konkani.

In recent years the forms $*-\bar{a}$, $*-\bar{\imath}$, and $*-\bar{u}$ have been reanalyzed
diachronically as originally consisting of a short vowel followed by
a laryngeal consonant. Upon the loss of this consonant, the preceding short vowel was lengthened. It is to this reconstructed laryngeal that the morphological function of forming collectives (and
abstracts) is to be ascribed. Of course, this same function was
assumed by the new long-vowel morphemes after the laryngeal disappeared. Thus, such an hypothesis has the distinct advantage of
explaining the functional equivalence of the three phonologically
different suffixes. I, too, believe that the long-vowel suffixes of
the feminine gender were originally composite; however, I maintain
that the second and primary member of the construction was the non-
singular desinence $*-N$.

As I have already indicated, the element $*-N$, as part of its general function as a non-singular marker, served the more specific
role of designating collectivity. Thus, collective formations involving the a-, i-, and u-stems were originally terminated in $*-aN$,
$*-iN$, and $*-uN$, later passing to $*-\bar{a}$, $*-\bar{\imath}$, and $*-\bar{u}$. Many of these
collectives then came to be reinterpreted as true singulars, desig-
nating individuals. By chance, a number of these new singulars in
$*-\bar{a}$, $*-\bar{\imath}$, and $*-\bar{u}$ referred to beings of the female sex; and $*-\bar{a}$,
$*-\bar{\imath}$, and $*-\bar{u}$ were segmented as female-signifying suffixes. The new
feminine declensional classes in $*-\bar{a}$, $*-\bar{\imath}$, and $*-\bar{u}$ gradually increased their size and developed a full system of inflections as a
result of analogical processes based on existing patterns and of
participation in inflectional innovations. Although traditional
diachronic theory links these three feminine markers with the neuter
plural morphemes, there is no formal or semantic reason why the
long-vowel non-singular endings of the dual and the plural of both
the animate and the inanimate declensions cannot be related to the

feminine suffixes in the same way, given the analysis which I have
presented.

It may be the case that a few examples of the prevocalic variant
of the old singularized collective in *-o-N from the animate declension survive into the dialects, although they were reanalyzed as
neuters. Thus, Brugmann (1904: 336-337) notes the existence of
neuter singular nouns terminated in *-oN with an original collective
meaning, which, interestingly enough, often stand beside alternate
forms terminated in *-ā: ". . . gr. ástron ai. tārā 'Sternbild,
Gestirn' zu astér "Stern', gr. phrátrā 'Brüderschaft' (ai. bhrātrá-m
Abstraktum 'Bruderschaft') zu ai. bhátar- 'Bruder', ai. tána-m taná
'Nachkommenschaft' zu tán- 'Ausbreitung, Fortpflanzung', lat. vallum
'Verschanzung' zu vallus 'Schanzpfahl'. Dazu Neutra mit Dehnstufen-
volkalismus, z.B. ai. sápta-m sāptá-m 'sieben in eins zusammenge-
fasst, Siebenzahl' (saptá), āsvá-m 'Pferdetrupp' (ásva-s), kāpóta-m
'Taubenschwarm' (kāpóta-s), ahd. huon nhd. huhn. . . ursprgl. 'Hähne
und Hennen zusammen', zu hano henna, ..." That these nouns were
generally assimilated into the neuter o-stems is not unexpected
since this nominal class is also terminated in a nasal in the nominative-accusative singular.

I further believe that *-N itself gradually came to have yet another secondary function, which was to derive abstract nouns from
verbs and adjectives. The semantic connection between this function
and that of indicating non-singularity has already been observed.
The use of the element *-N as a means of deriving abstract nouns
from verbs and adjectives is readily evidenced in the morpheme which
is generally reconstructed as *-mo-. This suffix frequently appears
in derived nouns together with an immediately preceding lengthened-
grade vowel: Skt. dhū-má-s 'smoke', Gk. thū-mó-s 'passion', Lat.
fū-mu-s, OCS dy-m-ъ 'smoke', Skt. bhā-ma-s 'light', Gk. khū-mó-s
'libation', Skt. hó-ma-s 'offering', Go. dō-m-s 'judgment'. It is
quite possible that such forms once again represent contaminations
of the two stem-alternates which resulted from the monophthongization of *-VN in preconsonantal position. The original suffix in
such forms was simply *-N, with the stem vowel *-o being added at a
later date as part of the general trend towards "the transference
of stems that do not end in -o or -ā . . . into the o- or ā-declen-
sion, without any modification of meaning" (Brugmann 1891: 110).
The substantially fewer forms with no lengthened-grade vowel, if one
does immediately precede the nasal suffix, simply represent reten-
tions of the prevocalic sandhi variants. The validity of this analysis is perhaps suggested by the fact that if no vowel immediately
precedes the suffix *-N, then lengthened-grade is not evidenced in
any vowel phoneme of the stem: Gk. pturmós 'sneezing', harpagmós

'booty', Skt. *idhmás* 'firewood'. Because of the apparent restric-
tions on the occurrence of the nasal marker in its non-singular
function, I maintain that only after the emergence of this suffix as
-No- was it utilized in deriving nouns from athematic verbs and adjectives.[8] However, it may be true that the constraints on distribution noted previously were relevant only to the non-singular
function of the suffix and not to its somewhat later use in this
secondary derivational capacity. Interestingly enough, a nasal element also appears in other suffixes used to derive abstract nouns:
-ni-, *-men-*, and *-no-*, cf. Brugmann 1904: 341-351. After the
passage of *-VN* to *-V̄*, many abstracts originally in *-N* similarly
came to comprise part of the new *ā-*, *ī-*, and *ū*-declensional classes.

Abstracts and collectives in *-ō* reinterpreted as singulars were
apparently eliminated because of their relative rarity. The assumed
scarcity of these forms is not as extraordinary as it first may appear if one accepts the fact that there was at one time a large *a*-
stem adjectival class. When the nominal *a-* and *ā*-stems underwent
assimilation, with the emergence of *-o* as a non-feminine stem-
formant, those adjectives that originally formed a non-feminine stem-
variant in *-a* and a feminine stem-variant in *-ā* merged the two
formations[9] and adopted *-o* as their non-feminine stem-forming element. Thus, they became identical in structure with the original
o-stem group. It is perhaps worth suggesting that such Greek relic
adjectival forms as *akámās* 'unwearied' and *argḗs* 'white', both with
a stem vowel originally in *-ā*, serving a generalized masculine-
feminine-neuter function, date from the time when the masculine-
neuter stem-variant in *-a* and the feminine stem-variant in *-ā* were
merged. The nominative ending *-s* may have resulted from the influence of the Greek masculine *ā*-stem nouns or from an early contamination of the original masculine ending *-as* (if it existed) with the
feminine suffix *-ā*. It is also possible that the general tendency
for *-ā* to replace *-ō* in the non-singular function brought about
such a substitution in the abstract function, thereby reducing the
number of singularized substantives in *-ō*. The apparent tendency
of the animate *o*-stems to preserve the prevocalic variant of the
suffix *-o-N* in collective function, which was liable to reanalysis
as a marker of the nominative-accusative singular neuter, may also
have been responsible for the relative rarity of these nouns.

Before concluding this section, I should comment on the chronology
of the developments described here in regard to the separation of
the Anatolian group from the main body of the Indo-European speech
community. I feel it is probable that Hittite inherited the results
of the monophthongization of *-VN* to *-V̄*. Indeed, Kuryłowicz says
that "the plural ending *-ă̄* of the neuter . . . is well attested in

Hittite" (1964: 217) and that a plural in *-$\bar{\imath}$ is suggested by a
number of forms (1958: 243), although the ambiguity of orthographic
evidence makes definitive analysis impossible. Of course, I firmly
maintain that the Anatolian group separated before the elements *-$\bar{a}$,
*-$\bar{\imath}$, and *-$\bar{u}$ were interpreted as feminine markers, thereby leading
to the creation of a specifically feminine gender.

4.4   The Subsequent Development of the Feminine Suffixes. Although
the feminine gender had its origin in the period when the unity of
the Indo-European speech community (excluding the Anatolian group)
was still a reality, it is probably true that the general extension
of the feminine markers, especially in nominal declension, occurred
primarily in the period of accelerated dialectal differentiation and
beyond. This statement is supported, for example, by the fact that
beside Skt. *áśvas* 'male horse', *áśvā* 'female horse'; Lat. *equus*
'male horse', *equa* 'female horse', is found the Greek masculine and
feminine form *híppos* 'horse'. Likewise, early Latin preserves in a
number of archaic formations an undifferentiated masculine-feminine
lupus 'wolf' (beside later *lupus* [masc.], *lupa* [fem.]), *agnus* 'lamb'
(beside later *agnus* [masc.], *agna* [fem.]), and *porcus* 'pig' (beside
later *porcus* [masc.], *porca* [fem.]), suggesting a very recent extension of the morpheme *-$\bar{a}$ in these nouns. That such extension continued to occur well within the historical period is clearly implied
by the existence of masculine-feminine *theós* 'god, goddess' in Attic
and Laconian Greek and the occurrence of the special feminine *theá*
'goddess' only in Homer (Meillet 1931: 26). Although in the various historical languages there exist a number of strong correspon-
dences of form and meaning involving feminine nominal forms, it must
be emphasized that the degree to which the extension of feminine
morphemes was a result of common, inter-dialectal, or independent
but parallel development is simply not possible to ascertain. The
last possibility could account for many cognate forms since the feminine construction is rather transparent morphologically. However,
I shall try at least to outline a sequence of changes which resulted
in the spread of the feminine suffixes.

    After the suffix *-$\bar{a}$ (and *-$\bar{\imath}$ and *-$\bar{u}$ as well) was interpreted as
an exponent of the semantic feature (Female), it then became a pro-
ductive element in the morphological system. I believe that its
productivity was at first limited to the adjectival class. Since
the adjective was an inherently variable form, it naturally served
as the vehicle through which the new morphological element could be
generally utilized. The new feminine adjective provided an especially simple and effective means of overtly specifying the sex of
what have come to be called nouns of the "common gender." Still

attested in the dialects, these nouns, which denote persons or animals, may be either masculine or feminine, depending on the inherent sex of their referents, with the adjective (or pronoun) alone indicating the gender class (i.e., they are invariable in form): e.g. Gk. *hîppos* 'horse', *aoidós* 'singer', *árktos* 'bear', *élaphos* 'deer', OCS *gostъ* 'stranger, guest', Skt. *gáus*, Lat. *bōs* 'bovine animal', OLat. *lupus* 'wolf', etc. Thus, in Greek the semantic opposition between 'a good male horse' and 'a good female horse' is expressed as *agathós hîppos* : *agathḗ hîppos*. Of course, before the appearance of the feminine morphemes, there existed no morphological means of indicating the sex of such nouns. The only way available was through lexical expression, i.e. modification by the adjective denoting 'male' or 'female', cf. Gk. *thêlus* 'female'. The replacement of a lexical sex-specification by a morphological one is quite in keeping with the general tendency in the historical development of Indo-European for morphology to expand at the expense of other levels of structure. Moreover, such clear and simple sex-specification became possible in situations involving the substantival use of adjectives, as in Fr. *les grandes* : *les grands*, where the indication of sex differences through further adjectival modification is somewhat awkward. Such considerations also led to the introduction of the morpheme *-ā* into the pronominal system, cf. *sā* 'she': Skt. *sā́*, Gk. *hḗ*, Go. *sō*.

It must be emphasized that the feminine suffixes in *-ī* and *-ū* (and, indeed, *-ā* for that matter) did not become productive in the *i*- and *u*-stem adjectives until a later date. This is demonstrated by Burrow's observation (1973: 204) that "the adjectives in *i* do not distinguish a masculine and feminine stem ([Skt.--K.S.] *śúcis* nom. sg. masc. and fem.) and those in *u* optionally follow the same system (*cā́rus* masc. and fem.). The latter may optionally form femininines in two ways (*bahvī́* 'much', *tanū́* 'thin'), but the fact that this still remains optional shows that it is a comparatively recent innovation." Fodor (1959: 38) suggests that "this phenomenon is explained by the fact that the improductive stems contained little used adjectives [at this stage of the language at least--K.S.]," which, because of their comparatively rare occurrence, did not generally develop the new variable terminations. Likewise, the consonant stem adjectives did not distinguish a masculine(-neuter) and a feminine stem until a later date—a fact demonstrated by significant dialectal differences in the extent of the differentiation in these adjectives and by the frequently imperfect nature of the differentiation within individual dialects, cf. Buck 1933: 210-211 and Kurylowicz 1964: 215.

The adjectival (at this point thematic stems only) use of the feminine morpheme was then generalized beyond the modification of those nominal forms where common gender was involved to all those nouns with the semantic feature (Female), e.g. Lat. *māter* 'mother'. Like the thematic nouns, the thematic adjectives adopted *-*ā* as the feminine stem-formant. Thus, the language came to possess a simple grammatical rule which specified that any thematic adjective (the most plentiful type after the *a*-stem adjectives merged with the *o*-stem adjectives) which modified an inherently female noun was constructed with the feminine morpheme *-*ā* as a stem-forming element, although a number of relic forms continue to retain an undifferentiated masculine-feminine stem into the historical period, e.g. Gk. *lábros* 'vehement', *tithasós* 'tame', *khérsos* 'unfruitful', etc. Archaic Latin texts clearly show an overlay of the new morphological and the older lexical means of sex-differentiation in common gender nouns in formations like *agnus fēmina* 'female lamb' and *lupus fēmina* 'female wolf'. Although the masculine and the neuter forms of the adjective shared a common stem, they were differentiated by inflectional patterns.

When used in a generic sense or in case the sex of the referent was irrelevant, these common gender nouns and their adjective modifiers continued to preserve the older (> masculine) construction. A few nouns of the common gender type in *-*ā* and *-*ī* are attested, but these are to be explained as original singularized abstracts and collectives that came to denote a particular species (and hence were not interpreted as specifically feminine). Since a number of nouns designating economically or socially unimportant animals, or creatures whose sex is extremely difficult to determine were rarely used in contexts where the specification of sex was essential, these forms eventually became crystallized in gender. In such cases, then, gender specification was manifested as essentially a formal rather than a logical linguistic entity. Thus, even when used in reference to specifically male or female beings, the gender of these so-called epicene nouns generally remained invariable, cf. Gk. *ho mûs* 'the mouse'. On those rare occasions when it became necessary to specify the sex of the referent of an epicene noun, lexical means were employed.

Once the productivity of the feminine suffix had become established within one part of the linguistic system (the thematic adjective and the pronoun), the suffix became similarly, though not nearly so thoroughly, productive in thematic nouns, thereby being extended beyond its original range of distribution in nominal declension. For example, the common gender noun *horse*, whose original character is still preserved in Gk. *híppos*, came to distinguish in

itself male and female through the adoption of *-$\bar{a}$ when it was used
in reference to a female: Lat. *equa*, Skt. *áśvā*, etc. Such generalization, which may have been largely dialectal, results from the
simple process of hypercharacterization. Thus, numerous constructions involving inherently female nouns terminated in *-$\bar{a}$, modified
by adjectival forms also terminated in *-$\bar{a}$ (and serving as antec-
dents for pronouns terminated in *-$\bar{a}$), came into existence.

The formal aspects of linguistic structure more strongly asserted
themselves at this point, and so further changes in the gender system took place. Many non-female, though singularized, nominal forms
terminated in *-$\bar{a}$, *-$\bar{\imath}$, and *-$\bar{u}$, whose original abstract and collective nature caused them to embody a wide variety of semantic proper-
ties, also came to be modified by the feminine form of the adjective
on analogy with genuine female nouns with these suffixes. The
formal aspects of the old system of gender classification (animate
vs. inanimate) encouraged such developments. (See Shields 1979a for
a discussion of additional factors which contribute to changes in
gender specification.) However, some frequently occurring lexical
items in *-$\bar{a}$ and *-$\bar{\imath}$ whose semantic structure was felt to be grossly
inconsistent with that of the formally identical members of the feminine gender class were generally excluded from membership in that
class; and some even changed their form in order to integrate themselves better into the gender class of which they were a part. Such
a state of affairs was responsible for the inclusion of Lat. *nauta*
'sailor', for example, in the class of masculine nouns and for the
adoption of the characteristic masculine nominative ending by this
form in Greek, i.e. *naútēs*. In addition, as part of this general
trend toward the adoption of feminine gender by nearly all nouns end-
ing in *-$\bar{a}$, *-$\bar{\imath}$, and *-$\bar{u}$, it seems that common gender nouns of these
stem classes came to adopt feminine gender markers (feminine forms
of the adjective and the pronoun) when they were used in a generic
sense or when the sex of their referents was simply ignored.

According to Kurylowicz (1964: 218), the feminine suffix *-$\bar{a}$
eventually tended to be ousted from nominal declension by the suffix
*-$\bar{\imath}$. That is, the morpheme *-$\bar{\imath}$ came to be interpreted as the pro-
ductive form. That this process at least had its start at a time
when the various Indo-European groups were still in fairly close
contact is suggested by the Sanskrit, Old Church Slavic, and Old Ice-
landic cognates *vr̥kī́s*,[10] *vlъči-ca*, and *ylgr* 'female wolf', although
independent but parallel development cannot be excluded. Thus, in a
real sense, ". . . the type *eku̯ā, the fem. of *ek̯u̯os (Skt. *áśvā*,
Lat. *equa*, Lith. *ašvà*) may be a derivational archaism, though of
course younger than Greek *ho híppos* : *hē híppos*" (Kurylowicz 1964:
218). A feminine form of the anaphoric(-demonstrative) pronoun in

*-$\bar{\imath}$ also arose from the interpretation of *-$\bar{\imath}$ as the productive feminine suffix (Go. si, OCS si, Skt. $sy\acute{\bar{a}}$ [< *$s\bar{\imath}$ + -$\bar{a}$]). Despite the fact that the suffix *-$\bar{\imath}$ tended to oust *-$\bar{a}$ from its position as the primary marker of the feminine gender in the substantive and the pronoun, *-$\bar{a}$ continued to function as the feminine marker in the thematic adjective. This is perhaps due to the crystallization of this morpheme in this function at an early date. However, the general trend of renewal continued even further in Sanskrit, where the newly productive suffix *-$\bar{\imath}$ spread to the thematic adjective, "entailing a stylistical difference between -$\bar{a}$- and -$\bar{\imath}$- in the fem. form" (Kurylowicz 1964: 218). That is, "Whether a masc.-neut. stem in -a shall form its feminine in $\bar{a}$ or in $\bar{\imath}$ is a question to be determined in great part only by actual usage, and not by grammatical rule" (Whitney 1973: 115)

It was perhaps during this time that *-$\bar{a}$ and *-$\bar{\imath}$ were contaminated to form the new feminine suffix *-$y\bar{a}$, cf. Kurylowicz 1964: 218. This new suffix *-$y\bar{a}$, as well as the now productive ending *-$\bar{\imath}$ with which it was associated as an ablaut variant,[11] was extended as a marker of the feminine to various non-thematic adjectival forms. In his description of this development, Martinet (1957: 87-88) says: "Le suffixe -$\bar{\imath}$-, -$y\bar{a}$- comme suffixe adjectival marquant le genre féminin: l'extension de ce suffixe pour former certains adjectifs féminins athématiques doit être nettement plus récente que l'apparition de ce suffixe et sa spécialisation pour les désignations d'êtres féminins; comme l'a bien marqué Meillet [(1931: 13-17)—K.S.], il n'y a pas accord d'une langue à une autre sur l'étendue et les modalités du phénomène." The generalization of *-$\bar{\imath}$, *-$y\bar{a}$ from the substantives to these adjectives was motivated by the following proportion (using Sanskrit forms):

substantive: $\acute{a}\acute{s}va$-s 'male horse'/ $\acute{a}\acute{s}v$-$\bar{a}$ 'female horse' : $r\bar{a}jan$- 'king'/ $r\bar{a}j\tilde{n}$-$\acute{\bar{\imath}}$ 'queen'

adjective: $n\acute{a}va$-s 'new'/ $n\acute{a}v$-$\bar{a}$ 'new' : $balin$- 'powerful'/ x

(Martinet 1957: 88). As to the date of this extension, Martinet (1957: 88) remarks: "Comme ces conditions existaient dans toutes les branches de la famille à date ancienne, un développement parallèle n'est nullement exclu; cependant, on ne saurait non plus écarter la possibilité que le processus ait été amorcé à une époque où, par exemple, Proto-Aryens et Proto-Grecs restaient en contact."

4.5   The Origin of the Germanic Weak Adjectival Declension. As a final point in my discussion of the origin and development of the non-singular number and the feminine gender in Indo-European, I wish

to suggest that the appearance of these categories is intimately related to the appearance of the weak adjectival declension in Germanic.

Of course, "The weak declension [of adjectives in Germanic--K.S.]
consists in the change of all adjective stems to *n*-stems—that is,
essentially in the addition of an *n*-determinant" (Prokosch 1939:
260). The weak form of the adjective occurs typically with the definite article (or similar definitivizing words), implying that the
original function of this "*n*-determinant" involved individualization,
whereas the strong form occurs in other environments, implying that
it originally possessed some kind of indefinite sense. After the
non-singular marker *-*N* was added to nouns in *-*a*, *-*o*, *-*i*, and *-*u*
in Indo-European, two sandhi variants developed: *-*V̄* (preconsonantal) and *-*VN* (prevocalic). It has been suggested that in the noun,
the preconsonantal variant gave rise to the feminine markers through
the processes of singularization and reanalysis, although its primary
function as a non-singular suffix is still widely attested in both
the originally animate and the neuter nouns. The same suffixes appear in the adjective as well since the noun tends to exert a strong
influence on it. Now in the dialects generally the old singularized
prevocalic variant has largely been lost in both the nouns and the
adjectives (or, in the nominal *o*-stem declension, at times reinterpreted as a neuter nominative-accusative singular suffix) because of
the generalization of the long-vowel suffix, which came to be an
exponent of the feminine singular. But apparently in the Germanic
dialects, there has been a significant preservation of both singularized variants in thematic adjectival declension, with a functional
specialization of these variants. The preconsonantal variant became
the feminine nominative singular of the strong declension (Go. *blinda*
'blind'); and the prevocalic variant, which shows singularization
but apparently not interpretation as feminine, was reanalyzed as an
n-stem formation and became the basis of the weak declension. Such
reinterpretation was a natural result of the fact that forms to which
the *-*N* non-singular marker was added originally served a generalized
non-singular function. Thus, when such original non-singular (collective) constructions were singularized, they readily appeared to
be *n*-stems, with a *-*∅* ending (nom. masc.-fem., nom.-acc. neut.).
The semantic value associated with the weak declension is simply a
result of the fact that the collective and the abstract functions of
*-*N* as well as the process of singularization in which it partici-
pated by definition imply definitization.[12]

Latin, too, shows a similar formation. In this regard Prokosch
(1939: 260) says: "The masc. adjectives could be changed to *n*-stems
to denote permanent quality, and these new stems formed proper names:
catus 'sly', *Catō, -ōnis* 'the sly one'; *rufus* 'red', *Rufō, -ōnis*

'Red-head'."   These substantives also attest to the use of *-N to
form abstract nouns and the tendency for such forms to undergo singularization, definitization, and reinterpretation as *n*-stems.   However, in Italic this formation apparently never gained the morphological and syntactic importance that it assumed in Germanic. Indeed,
the suffix appears here only as a minor component of the system of
nominal declension, deriving substantives from adjectives, not as a
productive adjectival formant serving as the exponent of an obligatory syntactic category.   A similar situation exists in a number of
other Indo-European languages.   Thus, Brugmann (1904: 339) cites
the following forms as examples of the construction: "Gr. *strábōn*
'Schieler' zu *strabós* 'schielend', *psólōn* 'Wollüstling' zu *psōlós*
'geil', *trḗrōn* 'Furchtsamer, Fürchtling' zu *trērós* 'furchtsam',
ouraniōn 'Himmlischer, Himmelsbewohner' zu *ouránios* 'himmlisch'. . .
Av. *marᵊtan-* 'Sterblicher' zu *marᵊta-* 'sterblich'.   Lit. *ruduõ* Gen.
rudeñs 'Herbst' ('Rotbraunner') zu *rùdas* 'rotbraun'.   Solche Bildun-
gen treten besonders als Personennamen auf, wie gr. *Strábōn*."

Thus, despite the fact that Prokosch and Brugmann were able to
see a connection between the Germanic weak adjectival declension and
these other forms, I believe that they were unable to see the scope
of the relationships among these and other constructions.   Moreover,
both scholars considered the substantivized adjectival formation to
be the source of the weak adjectives.   They suggest that the substantivized adjectives with the "*n*-determinant" developed an attri-
butive function and that this construction was then generalized.
Instead, I see the old secondary collective function of the non-singular marker *-N*, not its abstract function, to be the primary basis
of the weak adjectives.   This makes possible the elimination of the
posited change of substantive back to adjective since the adjective
would simply have assumed the *-N* suffix when it modified a non-
singular noun.[13]   And just as the thematic adjective acquired the
preconsonantal sandhi variant of the suffix which shows singularization and reinterpretation as a feminine marker (Go. nom. sg. fem.
blinda < *-ā̃*), so it acquired the prevocalic variant which showed
singularization, although the latter form was apparently eliminated
in most of the Indo-European dialects precisely because it took on
no specialized function there.

The widespread appearance of the weak construction in Germanic was
probably the result of the early emergence of the syntactic category
definite in the Germanic dialects themselves.   Of course, "The term
definiteness refers . . . to the act of attributing special significance to an object or quality viewed as a class" (Guild 1970: 162).
I believe that in Indo-European proper "definiteness was not indicated for nouns" (Lehmann 1974: 84), cf. Meillet 1964: 359-360,

although the importance of this category in Germanic is clearly illustrated by the fact that certain demonstrative stems came to function as definite articles in the Germanic dialects.[14] Moreover,
the development of the definite construction in *-N in the adjective
is not surprising since the adjective, by nature a noun-modifier, is
eminently equipped to serve as an exponent of the category. Indeed,
this adjectival means of indicating definiteness seems to predate
the use of the definite article, since the definite article as such
is attested only in West and North Germanic; "in Gothic, this development is not quite completed, but the trend is the same as in
WGmc." (Prokosch 1939: 267). This fact leads Meillet (1970: 102)
to conclude: "Indo-European . . . did not have an article. Common
Germanic did not have one either, and Gothic still did not have one
in the fourth century A.D. However, certain demonstratives before
nouns assumed a value that was increasingly accessory; in West Germanic it is the demonstrative OE. (acc.) ðone, OS. (nom.) thē, and
OHG. *der*, placed before the noun, and in Nordic it is the demonstrative -*enn*, placed after the noun and forming one body with it.
Thus the role of an accessory word such as the article increased
little by little, until the article became an essential element of
the language."

4.6   The Origin of the Endingless Locative. I would like to conclude the main body of my monograph with the presentation of an
analysis that assimilates many of the points made throughout the
book. In this way I hope to demonstrate how my approach can open up
possibilities for the reconstruction of Indo-European not heretofore
recognized. Specifically, I shall consider the origin of the endingless locative.

The endingless locative is a puzzling construction; for although
the emergence of an autonomous locative case was a late development
in Indo-European, the form of the endingless locative appears to be
very ancient indeed. This situation in part leads Benveniste (1935:
98-99) to conclude: ". . . ce que l'on dénomme 'locatif' repose
comme un bon nombre de nominatifs-accusatifs, sur un 'cas indéfini',
qui avait en indo-européen la forme même du thème neutre." Likewise, Hirt (1927: 48) says: "Der Lokativ ist . . . ursprünglich
endungslos gewesen. Er entspricht also dem Kasus indefinitus, und
er wird so, um mit Ludwig, Der Inf. im Veda, S. 9, zu reden, 'zu
einem Nachweis des Hereinragens der Epoche, wo die Sprache keine
Biegung kannte, in die Zeit vollständig ausgebildeter Flexion'."
However, on the basis of the analyses which I have presented so far,
an alternative hypothesis can be formulated which reconciles the

apparent archaic formal properties of the construction and its apparently recent functional properties.

Burrow (1973: 234) describes the endingless locative construction as follows: "The oldest form, the locative without ending, appears in *n*-stems (*áhan*, *mūrdhán*, *śīrṣán*; cf. Gk. *aién* 'always', and infinitives like *dómen*, etc.), and in the vṛddhied forms of the *i*- and *u*-stems. It also appears sporadically elsewhere, e.g. in *parút* 'last year' as opposed to Gk. *pérusi*, *péruti*, a compound whose last member (*-út*) is the weak form of the *wet* that appears in Hitt. *wett-*, Gk. *ɣétos* 'year'. In Avestan there appears a locative without ending from a root noun *man-* 'mind' in the phrase *mə̄n čа daidyāi* 'and to put in the mind, remember'."[15] In addition to this locative type, there appears in the singular of the historical dialects a formation in **-i* (< oblique **-i*), which is attested in all stem-classes, even those which show endingless forms as well, e.g. Skt. *vṛ́ke* 'wolf', Gk. *oíkoi* 'at home', Osc. *tereí* 'on the ground', etc.

Now there existed in Indo-European an *o*-stem locative (< oblique) construction which appears to have had two prevocalic sandhi variants, one in **-o-i* (Att. *oíkoi* 'at home', Lat. *hū-c* 'whither', OE *dæɜi* 'by day', OCS *vlъcě* 'wolf') and the other in **-e-i* (Att. *ekeî* 'there', Dor. *teî-de* 'here', *peî* 'where', Lat. *domī* 'at home', Osc. *múinikeí tereí* 'on common ground'). Phological developments in certain dialects prevent the determination of which variant is attested there: e.g. Skt. *vṛ́ke* (< **-oi* or **-ei*) 'wolf', OIr. *cinn* (< **kuennoi* or **-ei*) 'at the end', OLith. *dievie-p* (*-ie-* < **-oi* or **-ei*) 'with God'. I believe that traces of a preconsonantal sandhi variant in **-ē* (< **-oi*) continue to exist in that stem class. That the reconstruction of such a locative ending is by no means a novel idea is demonstrated by Brugmann's observation (1911: 175): "Einen gleichartigen Lok. auf **-ē* von *o*-Stämmen hat Walde Ausl. 7 ff. angenommen für den lit. Lok. auf *-e*, *vilkè*, und für die lokativisch gebrauchten ahd. *dorf* ags. *ham* u. dgl." Likewise, Hirt (1927: 48) says: "Im Litauischen lautet der Lok. *o*-Stämme *vilkè*, ... *è* muss aber doch wohl auf *é* zurückgehen. . . ."[16] The preconsonantal sandhi variant **-ī* (< **-ei*) has apparently disappeared from this declensional class in locative function. Of course, the formation in **-ē* (and similarly **-ī*) was reinterpreted as **-ē-∅*.

One frequently observes the extension of the endings of the *o*-stems to other stem classes. For example, in the instrumental singular Indo-Iranian attests the transfer of the *o*-stem ending *-ā* (< **-ō*) to the consonant stems (Skt. *śúnā* 'dog') (Brugmann 1911: 193-194), and in the instrumental plural Germanic shows a similar extension of the *o*-stem suffix to the consonant stems (Go. *gumam* 'men') (Brugmann 1911: 266). Likewise, Germanic *i*-stem genitive

singulars such as Go. *gastis*, OHG *gastes* 'guest' "zeigen den Ausgang
der *o*-Stämme, gleichwie im Dat. got. *gasta* ahd. *gaste*" (Brugmann
1911: 157). Italic and Avestan attest the extension of the ablative singular *o*-stem suffix in *-T* to other stem classes (Burrow
1973: 233), while the genitive (> genitive plural) suffix found in
all stem classes (*-ŏN*) probably has its origin in the *o*-stems
(Schmalstieg 1977b: 130).

I believe that the rarity with which the preconsonantal sandhi
variants *-ē* and *-ī* seem to appear in the *o*-stem class is a result
of the fact that they were largely transferred to and subsequently
specialized in other declensional classes. The suffix *-ī* seems to
have come to mark the locative singular in the consonant stem nouns,
although it generally disappeared there as well, yielding to other
formations. Thus, Meillet (1964: 295) says: "En latin, la forme
qui conserve un type spécial de locatif est en *-ī*: *Karthagin-ī*."
Brugmann (1893: 157) also notes that "along with *-i* we have *-ī* in
Greek and Sanskrit, Hom. *patér-ī* and the like. . . , Ved. *vaktár-ī*
and the like. . . ." [17] The suffix *-ē*, on the other hand, came to
be specialized largely in the *-i* and *u*-stems: Ved. *ávā* (*ávis*
'snake'), *agnā́* (*agnís* 'fire'), Hom. *pólēi* (< *-ē* contaminated with
the locative suffix *-i*) (*pólis* 'city'), OIr. *fáith* (< *-ē* or *ēi*)
(*fáith* < *u̯ātis* 'seer'), Go. *anstai* (< *-ēi*) (*ansts* 'favor'), OCS
nošti (< *-ēi*) (*noštь* 'night'), Skt. *sūnāú* (< *-ē* contaminated with
the particle *-u*) (*sūnús* 'son'), Lat. *noctū* (< *-ēu*) (adv. 'by
night'), Go. *sunau* (< *-ēu*) (*sunus* 'son'), OCS *synu* (< *-ou* < *-eu* <
-ēu) (*synъ* 'son'). [18] The extension of *-ē* (and similarly *-ī*) to
these declensions was motivated by the following proportion:

> Noun-*o*-Ending : Noun-*ē*-Ending (*-∅)
> Noun-*i*-Ending : Noun-*ē*-Ending (*-∅)

That is, since *-ē* had already been interpreted as a stem-forming
element with a *-∅ ending, it was appropriate that it came to serve
the same function in the *i*- and *u*-stems. It was important for the
entire stem-formation to be transferred because the marker *-∅ alone
would not have characterized the construction precisely enough. Its
appearance, for example, in the nominative-accusative singular neuter demonstrates this fact.

Now during the time of the formation of the endingless locative,
ablaut was becoming an important morphological indicator in the language, although it is probably true that its development, especially
in regard to lengthened grade (which was frequently the result of
the monophthongization of preconsonantal diphthongs in word-final
position), had not yet reached the level of complexity attested in
the historical dialects themselves. In any event, the analogically

extended *o*-stem suffix *-$\bar{e}$, contaminated with the elements *-*i* and *-*u*, came eventually to be interpreted as a vṛddhied form of the stem-formant of the *i*- and *u*-stems, just as the suffix *-$\bar{e}$ probably came to be interpreted as a lengthened-grade form of the stem-element in the *o*-stems, although its rarity in attested lexical items prohibits definitive analysis. However, the secondary character of this suffix in the locative singular of the *i*- and *u*-stems is perhaps evidenced by the fact that the vṛddhied form of the stem-element is not usual there. As Meillet (1964: 307-308) says about athematic declension, "Le locatif singulier a un vocalisme prédésinentiel caractéristique: voyelle brève *e*, ainsi dans skr. *netár-i* 'chez le conducteur' avec *a* représentant *e* . . . ; de même le locatif véd. *dyáv-i* 'au ciel', identique à lat. *Iou-e* (de *dyew-i*), s'oppose au génitif à vocalisme prédésinentiel zéro véd. *div-áḥ*, cf. gr. *Diϝ-ós*."[19] In thematic declension, with the exception of the relic suffix *-$\bar{e}$, one sees the *o*-grade or the *e*-grade of the stem vowel, cf. Meillet 1964: 322-323. Vṛddhied forms thus appear generally in endingless locatives of the *i*- and *u*-stems and in a few other isolated formations, e.g. Greek adverbs of the type *núktōr* 'by night', etc. The analogical origin of some of these will be discussed below.

I believe, cf. Kurylowicz 1964: 195-200, that the suffix *-*i* is far more ancient in locative function in the *i*- and *u*-stems than *-$\emptyset$, although *-*i* was largely replaced in these classes by *-$\emptyset$. But traces of this older construction continue to exist in these declensional types well into the historical period. The *i*-stems seem to show it in such dialectal forms as Hom. *pósei*, *póseï* (< *-*ei*-i*) 'husband',[20] Att. *pólei* (< *-*ei*-i*) 'city', Osc. *Fuutreí* (< *-*ei*-i*) 'Genetricī', and perhaps Ved. *ājáyi* (< *-*ei*-i*) 'contest', despite the fact that the retention of *-*i*- in Sanskrit is unexpected in this phonological environment, cf. Brugmann 1904: 92. Brugmann (1911: 182) suggests therefore that this Vedic locative formation is "eine Neubildung," as do Wackernagel and Debrunner (1896: 199); but if this latter word and the very few like it (see Wackernagel and Debrunner 1930: 154 in this regard) are relic forms, then the retention of *-*i*- may be explained simply as a case of residue. The validity of this hypothesis is perhaps suggested by Sihler's conclusion (1977: 6) that "in medial sequences . . . the loss of *y* before *i* . . . took place either just prior to or concurrent with the early Vedic period." The *u*-stems also clearly attest a locative construction in *-*i*: Hom. *hēdéï* (< *-*eu*-i*) 'sweet', Att. *dorí* (< *dorϝi*) 'wood, spear', Ved. *sūnávi* (< *-*eu*-i*) 'son', and perhaps ORuss. *domovъ* (< PS *domovъ*) 'home', cf. Brugmann 1911: 182. The consonant stems give quite definitive evidence of the antiquity of

this construction, e.g. *n*-stems: **-en-i*, Go. *hanin* 'cock', Skt.
mūrdháni 'head', Gk. *poiméni* 'shepherd', Lat. *homine* 'man'; *r*-stems:
*-er-i, Skt. *mātári*, Hom. *mētéri* 'mother', Armen. *dster* 'daughter'.
The problem remains, however, to explain the development of the endingless locative formation in nouns of this type.

The appearance of a **-∅* ending in locative function in nouns like
these crucially involved the development of nominative in **-V̄(C)* (as
opposed to vocatives in **-VC*) in animate consonant stems and of nominative-accusative non-singulars (> plurals) in **-V̄(C)* (as opposed
to nominative-accusative singulars in **-VC*) in neuter consonant
stems through monophthongization. Now in the animate consonant
stems, the old prevocalic variant did, in a general sense, come to
assume the vocative function. But because of the peculiar accentual
pattern which the vocative had developed,[21] it remained phonologically (i.e. suprasegmentally) distinct from the old nominative (i.e.
nom. **pətér* vs. voc. **péter*). I would like to suggest that the prevocalic variant which served as the old nominative apart from the
vocative became reinterpreted as a locative. The motivation for
this reanalysis was provided by the fact that it shared a **-∅* ending
with the locative of *o-*, *i-*, and *u*-stems (and it frequently shared
the position of the accent with them as well). That linguistic
change is by nature a gradual and variable process explains the continued existence of the variant for some time, an obvious prerequi-
site for reanalysis. The neuter consonant stem nouns retained the
prevocalic variant in the nominative-accusative singular, but this
sandhi variant tended to assume the locative function on analogy
with the animate nouns. This natural analogical pressure was aug-
mented by the fact that the accusative case itself had a secondary
locative function (inherited from its origin in the objective case),
which Brugmann (1904: 442) describes as "Der Akk. der Räum- oder
Zeiterstreckung." Likewise, Hirt (1934: 34) suggests that there
existed in later Indo-European and in the dialects an "Akkusativ der
Zeit" (cf. Kurylowicz 1964: 182, where this function is referred to
as "Acc. of temporal extension"): "So heisst es gr. *próter-on*
gegenüber ai. *prātar* 'früh', gr. *authémeron* gegenüber *hêmar*; ai.
náktam neben *divā́*. Dieses *naktam* und ähnliche Fälle haben dann
weitergewuchert und einen Akk. der Zeit hervorgerufen. Vgl. ai. *tạ*
purvē-djuḥ (Lok.) *pitarō vindann, uttaram ahar* (Akk.) *dēvāḥ* 'am vor-
hergehenden Tag fanden ihn die Väter, am folgenden die Götter'."
He similarly posits an "Akk. des Ortes . . . z.B. l. *dom-um ire*
'nach Hause gehen'; ai. *dūr-ám* 'in die Ferne', gr. *apékhei d' hē*
Plátaia tôn Thēbôn stadíous hebdomékonta 'Plataia ist von Theben 70
Stadien entfernt'" (Hirt 1934: 35) (cf. Kurylowicz 1964: 182 in
regard to "Acc. of spatial extension"). However, these consonant

stem endingless locative forms, because of their homophony with the
nominative-accusative singular neuter, never really did gain much of
a foothold in the language, as the rarity of attested forms indicates.
Thus, Burrow's statement (1973: 244) in regard to the *r*-stems that
"no forms of the loc. sg. without ending are preserved, though such
presumably existed at one time" must be rethought: the lack of
forms is not to be attributed to the disappearance of an archaic
formation but to the inability of an innovation to become adopted
generally.

Additional analogical changes involving the endingless locative
formations should be mentioned in closing. The lengthened grade of
the locative singular of the *o-*, *i-*, and *u*-stems tended to exert analogical pressure on the new endingless forms of the consonant stems,
resulting in the appearance of such forms as Avest. *ayąn* (< *-ēn*)
'day', OPers. *namā* (< *-ēn*) 'name', and perhaps OIr. *toimte* (<*-tiōn*)
'opinion'. In the *i*-stems the *-i-* of forms like Skt. *pátyāu* 'husband' probably results from the influence of the dative (*pátyē*) and
the instrumental (*pátyā*) (Brugmann 1911: 176). Although the *-u*
here is frequently explained as a transfer from the *u*-stems, I prefer
to see it as an original particle in *-u*. It also appears in *i*-stem
forms such as *agnāú* 'fire' (without the *-y-*). *u*-stem forms like Skt.
vástō 'with flashing', Avest. *daⁱŋhō* (< *-eu*) 'province' are analogical formations showing the normal grade of the stem-element like
other classes, e.g. Skt. *pitár-i* 'father'. *i*-stem forms like Avest.
garō 'mountain' show a transfer of *-ō* from the *u*-stems (Brugmann
1911: 175).

NOTES

[1]As Petersen (1939: 78) observes: "The palatal *-ñ* implies the loss
of a following palatal vowel. . . ." Although he suggests that this
vowel was originally the *-e* of the plural ending *-es*, I believe
that the non-singular suffix *-i* was the relevant phoneme here, occurring in contamination with *-N*.

[2]Of course, as I suggested earlier, the long vowel of these oblique
forms may be derived from the passage of an objective construction
in *-oN* to *-ō*. Moreover, as I also mentioned before, the particular
case distinctions made within the non-singular reflect early etymological connections among the case categories. It would seem that
during the period of the formation of the non-singular categories,
functional distinctions among many of the oblique cases had not yet
crystallized. That is, the identity of the dative, ablative, and
instrumental in the dual implies that these three cases were not yet
fully autonomous entities when the dual number was emerging.

[3]As far as Hittite is concerned, I assume that the original neuters
in *-a* adopted the *-N* of the *o*-stem class, after the passage of *o*
to *a* in this language.

[4]On the origin of Go. *-a*, see below. Of course, Germanic shows
the lengthened grade of the suffix in the nominative-accusative sin-

gular of the neuter n-stems (Go. *namō* 'name', *hairtō* 'heart'), as do
Slavic (OCS *jimę* 'name') and perhaps Baltic (Lith. *šelmuõ* 'gable'),
cf. Brugmann 1911: 145. I believe that these forms are all original
non-singulars reinterpreted as singulars. I have already demonstrated that a great deal of vacillation in number specification existed in the neuter consonant stems well into the historical period;
and this fact, together with the contamination of these original
non-singular constructions with other non-singular markers, e.g. Go.
hairtōna = *hairtō*(*n*) (= plural) + -*a* (= plural), make reinterpretation easily possible, i.e. Go. *hairtō*(*n*) (= singular) + -*a*(= plural).
The lengthened-grade of the nominative case of the masculine-feminine
n-stems may also have exerted some analogical pressure for the development of this formation. The n-stem nominative-accusative neuter
singular in *-ṇ* (Skt. *nāma*, Gk. *ónoma*, Lat. *nōmen* 'name') is simply
an alternate stem-form (the so-called weak grade). This stem-alter-
nate was apparently generalized at the expense of the original form
in *-Vn* in these dialects, just as the stem-element in *-V̄n* was in
Germanic and Balto-Slavic. This extension was probably the result
of the full emergence of the system of ablaut, in which "le nominatif-
vocatif-accusatif neutre singulier a d'ordinaire le vocalisme zéro
de l'élément prédésinentiel (la désinence étant zéro)" (Meillet 1964:
306), cf. especially i-stems like Skt. *ákṣi* 'eye', Gk. *ídri* 'clever',
etc. and u-stems like Skt. *mádhu* 'honey', Gk. *méthu* 'intoxicating
drink', etc.

[5]The origin of vocalic nasalization in such forms, I believe, stems
from the influence of the original nasal non-singular marker; however, the construction still remains largely enigmatic. Brugmann
(1904: 393) simply observes: "Die Nasalierung in ai. *várcąsi*,
ásiyąsi, *vidvą́si* war ind. Neurung." An explanation involving analogical pressures exerted by the n- and nt-stems has become popular.
See Thumb and Hauschild 1959: 106-107 for a clear presentation of
this position. It should be noted that "a non-nasalized form remains
only in the case of *catvā́ri* 'four'" (Burrow 1973: 238). That analogy
does, however, operate here in some way to extend the nasal marker
is suggested by the fact that the nasalized form spreads "further in
the post-Ṛgvedic period by the creation of nasalized i-plurals for
consonantal root-stems, e.g. *śaṅki* from *śak-* 'able', *bundhi* from
budh- 'understanding'. . . . Furthermore, . . . the later language
creates a neut. pl. -*tṝṇi* for stems in -*tṛ*" (Burrow 1973: 238). I
believe that this latter ending was created on analogy with the o-,
i-, and u-stem neuter plural suffix -*V̄ni*.

[6]See Burrow 1949, 1973: 106-197, 1979, Wyatt 1970, and Shields
1980d, Forthcoming b in this regard. As Burrow (1973: 106) says:
"If this ə had been confined to the comparatively few words in which
Sanskrit i appeared to correspond to a in the other languages, it
would never have acquired very great importance in Indo-European
theory. It was due to its becoming a basic element in the early
theories of apophony that it acquired such importance in the traditional theory of Indo-European."

[7]The suffix *-yā̄* is simply a contamination of *-ī̄* and *-ā̄*: *-(*i*)*yā̄*
< *-ī̄* + -*ā* (Kurylowicz 1964: 218).

[8]This state of affairs is also suggested by the fact that from
very ancient times, the simple vocalic suffixes *-*o*- and *-*a*- (later
*-*ā*-) were generally used to derive abstract nouns from athematic
verbs and adjectives: Gk. *khróm-o-s* 'noise', *gón-o-s* 'birth',
phug-ḗ 'flight', Skt. *jā́n-a-m* 'birth', Lith. *srav-ã* 'bleeding', OCS
oblak-ʒ 'cloud'.

[9]As Kurylowicz (1964: 217) notes: "The general rule for the inflection of the adjective is that it is at any moment liable to undergo the influence of the noun."

[10]As this form indicates, Sanskrit attests to a tendency to general-
ize the nominative marker *-s* to the $\bar{\imath}$-stem class. Although the

$\bar{\imath}$-stems only sporadically adopted this ending, Greek and Sanskrit evidence demonstrates that the $\bar{u}$-stem class of nouns without exception came to use it as an indicator of the nominative. I should also point out that the newly productive feminine suffix $*\text{-}\bar{\imath}$ was extended to certain non-thematic stem nouns (cf. Skt. *rajñī́* 'queen', *jánitrī* 'female ancestor') at this time, resulting in an increase in the size of the original $\bar{\imath}$-stem group.

[11] I would suggest that nouns like Skt. *kanyā́* 'girl', Go. *brakja* 'strife', OCS *duša* 'soul', etc. represent items in which the normal grade variant $*\text{-}y\bar{a}$ of the suffix $*\text{-}\bar{\imath}/\text{-}y\bar{a}$ has come to be generalized throughout their declension. Following the appearance of $*\text{-}y\bar{a}$ in these new environments, nouns of this type were inflected in the same fashion as simple $\bar{a}$-stems, cf. Schmalstieg 1973: 146.

[12] The $*\text{-}\breve{V}N$ formation adopted the long vowel of the n-stems where appropriate, e.g. Go. nom. sg. masc. *blinda* ($< *\text{-}\bar{o}n$), a development motivated by analogy and perhaps by the contamination of sandhi variants ($*\text{-}on + *\text{-}\bar{o} > *\text{-}\bar{o}n$). That the singularized thematic adjectives in $*\text{-}N$ did not undergo the same reanalysis as the singularized o-stem nouns in $*\text{-}N$ is a result of the fact that the gender of the adjective is dependent upon that of the noun modified; it is not inherent in the adjective itself. Thus, adjectives of this type were analogically viewed as part of a general stem-class, the n-stems. Interestingly enough, as the Latin, Greek, Avestan, and Lithuanian forms cited immediately below indicate, this same reanalysis is attested in nominal declension. Of course, this is not surprising since the inherent surface ambiguity here permits alternate reinterpretations.

[13] Although I do not find the hypothesis of Prokosch and Brugmann to be a particularly satisfying one, I frankly admit that it cannot be disproven. A more interesting alternative proposal is made by Hirt (1932: 99), who considers the n-determinant to be "das postponierte Pronomen *en* (slaw. *onŭ*), das im Sinn des Artikels steht, genau wie im Lit. Slaw. *-is*, *-jo* postponiert ist, lit. *geràs-is*, abg. *dobrŭjĭ*." As Prokosch (1939: 307) observes: "This seems quite plausible, but it is hardly possible to prove it." Lehmann (1970) propounds a view similar to that of Hirt, although his arguments are presented in terms of typological considerations, i.e., ". . . the weak inflections provide further insights into changes which took place as IE dialects moved to a VO structure" (1974: 246). He says "In this inflection the relative marker of reduced relative clauses was maintained as a suffix in Slavic and Baltic, e.g., OCS *vino novoje* 'wine (which is) new', in contrast with *vino novo* 'new wine', and Lith. *geràsis* 'the good one' as opposed to *gěras* 'good'. The weak or definite forms of adjectives can be accounted for through their reduction from relative constructions, in contrast with the strong declensions, which continue the regular IE adjective inflection. . . . Germanic, which lacked reflexes of the *yo* marker, generalized the *n* inflection for definite adjectives" (1974: 245-246). Despite the fact that he posits no direct source for the Germanic n-determinant, he concludes: "Accordingly we may relate syntactically the Germanic weak adjective inflection and the definite adjective inflections of Baltic and Slavic, though they are marked by different morphological means" (1970: 289). However, Guild (1970) presents strong evidence that the pronominal form $*\text{-}yo\text{-}$ found in the Baltic and Slavic declensions is a deictic element, not a relative, thereby demonstrating the close relationship of the definite article of South Slavic (Bulgarian and Macedonian) and the definite adjectival declension. Furthermore, he says that "in Lithuanian *jis*, *ji* is also found as the pronoun of the third person and the association between the two uses of an original deictic is very clear" (1970: 170). Likewise, Ard (1977: 8-25) directly points up problems in Lehmann's analysis of the origin of the definite adjectives in Baltic and Slavic, suggesting finally that "the immediate source of definite adjectives then was a structure involving a definitizing clitic which

developed from a demonstrative. . . " (1977: 22). These remarks
lead one to recall Jeffers' comments (1976: 986) regarding Lehmann's
general approach to linguistic change: "Hypotheses based on typological considerations should be made to fit the facts; but in some
cases, at least, Lehmann has seen fit to view the facts only in light
of the demands made by specific typological considerations. This is
unfortunate. The typological possibilities offer considerable lati-
tude, but facts must be confronted at face value." Yet, again it is
impossible to disprove completely what Lehmann has suggested. Thus,
it is once again my goal to propose another plausible explanation
of the origin of the formation in question, not to assert that my
hypothesis is the only possible one.

[14] In regard to the appearance of the definite article, it should
be emphasized that "comparable developments took place in other languages, in Greek from an early date, in Romance, in Celtic, and in
Armenian" (Meillet 1970: 102). But despite the fact that the development of the category of definiteness is evident in other Indo-
European dialects, "Nowhere is it more strongly manifested than in
the Germanic languages" (Meillet 1970: 102).

[15] Brugmann (1911: 174) says that the endingless locative "erscheint
bei Stämmen auf -*i*, -*u*, Nasal, Liquida, -*s*."

[16] Endzelīns (1971: 135) argues that the Lithuanian suffix "developed from an acuted -*en*," but this is not a necessary assumption.

[17] Wackernagel and Debrunner (1930: 207) are uncertain about the
origin of this long-vowel suffix. They note that "metrisch gedehntes
-*tarī* ist möglich," although "doch kann es an den in Betracht kommen-
den Stellen auch als NASg. Neutr. gefasst werden." Perhaps this
ending is also attested in the *i*-stems of Sanskrt, since Whitney
(1973: 117) observes: "Half-a-dozen locatives in *ī* . . . are made
from *i*-stems," e.g. *vēdī* 'place of sacrifice'. But these very rare
forms may be better explained in other ways, cf. Wackernagel and
Debrunner 1930: 154-155. The Latin forms in -*ī* (which alternate
with those in -*e* [< *-*i*]) are generally explained as showing the
specifically Latin sporadic transfer of the *o*-stem ending (OLat. -*ei*
> -*ī*) to the consonant stems, cf. Buck 1933: 186; but this is not a
necessary explanation.

[18] Brugmann (1904: 88) suggests that the simple *-*ē* found in some
of these forms results from the fact that "schon im Uridg. müssen
unter gewissen Bedingungen *i* und *u* in den Langdiphthongen geschwunden
sein."

[19] Burrow (1973: 234) further explains: "The [locative--K.S.] type
akṣṇí is the latest. According to the grammarians the locative of
n-stems may be in -*ani* or -*ni* (*rájani, rájñi; sakthán i, sakthní*),
but in the language of the Ṛgveda the latter type does not appear,
and is therefore clearly an innovation. It is due to an analogical
tendency to put the loc. sg. on the same footing as the other oblique
cases by accenting the termination and weakening the suffix. In many
of the consonantal stems this tendency had already become general in
the pre-Vedic period (*adati, bhágavati, vidúṣi*, etc.), but the older
type with accent and guṇa of the suffix is preserved in the *an*-stems,
in *r*-stems (*svásari, pitári*), to which certain monosyllabic stems
can be added: *kṣámi, dyávi* (beside *diví*)."

[20] The stem-formant *-*ei*- is attested elsewhere in the *i*-stems,
just as *-*eu*- is attested elsewhere in the *u*-stems: these so-called
strong-grade forms also "appear in the gen. sg. and voc. sg., and in
. . . the dat. sg., . . . , and nom. pl." (Buck 1933: 173). However,
only the locative singular shows the lengthened grade in *-*ēi*- and
*-*eu*-.

[21] As Brugmann (1904: 377) explains: "Der Vok. war ohne Kasus-
formans. An der Spitze des Satzes stehend war er uridg. orthoton
mit Accent auf der ersten Silbe, z.B. ai. *pítar*, gr. *páter* 'O, Vater';

daher noch mit vollstufiger erster Silbe ai. *sántya* Vok. zu *satyá-s*
'wahrhaft, treu'. . . . Sonst war der Vok. unbetont, z.B. ai. *idám*
indra śŗņuhi 'dies, Indra, höre'."

[22]It is possible that such *r*-stem forms, though rare, did exist.
Traces of the formation may be seen, e.g., in Skt. *áhar-divi* 'day by
day', "which is naturally associated with non-nominal forms such as
Skr. *antár* 'inside, inwards' (beside *antári-kṣa-*) Lat. *inter*, Gk.
húper Lat. *s-uper*" (Brugmann 1893: 159).

5 A Brief Chronological Summary

5.   Since my presentation of material has, of logical necessity, been organized in both a topical and a chronological fashion, the sequencing of changes occurring in the Indo-European declensional system is not always easy to follow. Therefore, I would like to conclude with a brief outline of the important stages through which the Indo-European language evolved, beginning with that stage of development when ergative structure was predominant. The stages, as I have defined them, are arbitrary; but they provide a useful framework in which to proceed.

5.1   Stage I. Although originally Indo-European was probably an isolating language, its earliest inflectional elements in the noun were ergative suffixes in *-∅ and *-r, and an absolute suffix in *-N. Nominal classes were at this time semantically defined—inanimate, animate, and natural agent—with only the last two classes generally appearing in the ergative case. An assonance concord system was in existence, although there was no formal agreement between subjects and verbs.

5.2   Stage II. Indo-European became a nominative-accusative language through the development of an assonance concord relationship between the ergative in *-∅ and the non-personal verbal suffix *-∅. After *-∅ was generalized as an indicator of animate and natural agent subject in intransitive sentences, the language came to have a nominative case in *-∅ and an objective case in *-N. This objective case had the functions of the historical accusative, dative, instrumental, genitive, ablative, and locative, while the nominative case marked the vocative function as well as the nominative. The nominal classes began to lose their semantic motivation and to acquire formal characteristics, first as a result of the mixing of the inanimates and the natural agents, and then as a result of the mixing of all three. Nevertheless, three distinct inflectional

patterns remained in nominal declension: an animate with a nominative in *-∅ and an objective in *-N, an inanimate with a nominative
and an objective in *-N, and a natural agent with a nominative and
an objective in *-∅. Assonance concord was still prominent in the
language, although it was less systematic than it once was.

5.3 Stage III. At the beginning of this period, the declensional
system saw the emergence of an oblique case which was marked by a
number of new inflectional elements with an adverbial origin (*-s,
*-i, and probably *-T), although the old objective suffix *-N was
also used as an exponent of this case, in addition to its indicating
the accusative. A separate vocative form developed in the animate
o-, i-, and u-stems; and near the end of Stage III, enclitic adverbs
(*-N and probably *-i) began to appear optionally on nominal forms
as indicators of non-singularity. A new nominative marker in *-s,
of verbal origin, also began to come into competition with *-∅ in
the animate nouns. By the end of this stage, only two classes of
nouns—animates and inanimates (neuters)—were in evidence since the
*-∅ suffix of the nominative-accusative of the old natural agents
was gradually generalized to all inanimate and natural agent stem-
classes except o-stems, which showed the old specifically inanimate
nominative-accusative suffix *-N. In spite of the ever-increasing
influence of traditional concord, assonance concord remained the
primary type of agreement during this time. Ablaut had its begin-
nings in this stage, although such variations were largely perceived
as stem-alternates with no morphological function. The vocative
formation did, of course, have morphologically significant vocalic
alternations; so perhaps it served as the basis for the development
of the historical ablaut system.

5.4 Stage IV. During this stage, which can in part be equated
with what is traditionally called Proto-Indo-European, dialectal
differentiation began to accelerate. This was especially true near
the end of the period. Two important phonological developments took
place at this time. Near the beginning of Stage IV, various monophthongizations of preconsonantal diphthongs in word-final position
began to occur; and not long afterwards accent started to become
morphologically, instead of syntactically, conditioned. The nominative (singular) animate suffix *-s came to be firmly established
during this period (but not before the r-, l-, m-, and n-stems had
largely developed nominatives in *-V̄(R)), resulting in the limitation of the functions performed by the oblique suffix *-s. The merger of the new nominative in *-s and the genitive in *-s was short-
lived because of the gradual development of morphologically condi-

tioned accent. Special vocative forms appeared in the animate nouns
of the consonant stems, and *-*bh* was introduced as an oblique-case
marker, though it did not become productive in nominal declension at
this time. The dative, instrumental, locative, ablative, and, especially, genitive cases began gradually to emerge as autonomous entities from the old oblique case through the specialization of suffixes or combinations of suffixes, and the specialization of contaminated forms, although a great deal of formal and functional over-
lapping among the oblique cases continued into the historical period.
In general terms, the dative and the instrumental utilized *-*N* (or
its monophthongized variant), *-*i*, and, to a far lesser extent, *-*T*
as their exponents, while the locative showed *-*i* as its primary
marker and *-*s* in contamination with other elements as a very important secondary indicator. *-*N* also appeared frequently in this
function, and *-*T* probably was used sporadically as a locative desinence. The genitive employed *-*s* and *-*N* as its primary exponents
and *-*i* as a secondary one. The ablative, which remained closely
associated with the genitive, utilized *-*T* as its primary suffix
along with *-*N* (and its preconsonantal sandhi form) and *-*s*, which
it shared with the genitive. Further differentiation among the
cases was also precipitated by the emergence of ablaut as an important morphological indicator during this stage. Well into this
period, the generalized non-singular construction, marked by *-*N* (or
its monophthongized form), *-*i*, and *-*s* (which probably appeared
during Stage IV), began to develop more case distinctions, even
though the non-singular category was still not an obligatory one.
The endingless locative fully emerged at the very end of Stage IV,
just before the split of the Anatolian group, since Hittite shows
only meager traces of this formation, cf. Friedrich 1974: 44. Likewise, the fact that the dual number is only primitively developed
in Hittite, cf. Sturtevant 1933: 165, implies that the bifurcation
of the non-singular into dual and plural occurred near the end of
Stage IV. With the establishment of *-*s* as a nominative suffix in
animate nouns, the demise of the assonance concord system was complete; and traditional concord emerged as the primary means of indicating agreement.

5.5   Stage V.   This was the stage during which highly accelerated
dialectal differentiation occurred. It was characterized by the
further formal and functional differentiation of the oblique cases
and the cases of the dual and the plural, as well as by the emergence of the feminine gender and its subsequent generalization (which
continued well into the era of the individual dialects). The case

marker *-*bh* became a productive element of the system of nominal
declension in certain dialect groups during Stage V.

5.6   What I have proposed in the preceding pages is a model of the
evolution of the Indo-European system of nominal inflection—a model
based on a number of reasonable assumptions: (1) the validity of
the sociolinguistic approach to language change, (2) the plausibil-
ity of Schmalstieg's theory of Indo-European monophthongizations,
and (3) the importance of non-proportional analogy in the historical
development of natural languages.   However, I wish to reiterate that
Indo-European did not necessarily evolve in the way that I have
described it since the data analyzed here are subject to variant
interpretations.   But because of this ambiguity, I want to emphasize
that Indo-European may very well have undergone the changes which
I have posited.   In the final analysis, we linguists, as mere mor-
tals, are forced to ask the same question as Pilate—"And what is
truth?"—but since Divine Revelation says nothing about the structure of the Indo-European language, we can only speculate.

References

Adrados, Francisco. 1971. "On Indo-European Sigmatic Verbal Stems."
Archivum Linguisticum 2: 95-116.

—————. 1975. *Lingüística indoeuropea*. Vol. 1. Madrid:
Gredos.

Andersen, Henning. 1973. "Abductive and Deductive Change." *Language* 49: 765-793.

Anttila, Raimo. 1972. *An Introduction to Historical and Comparative Linguistics*. New York: The Macmillan Co.

—————. 1973. "Was There a Generative Historical Linguistics?"
The Second International Conference of Nordic and General Linguistics, Umeå, Sweden, June 14-19, 1973.

Ard, William. 1977. "Methodological Problems in the Use of Typologies in Diachronic Syntax." Bloomington: Indiana University
Linguistics Club Publications.

Aronson, Howard. 1970. "Towards a Semantic Analysis of Case and
Subject in Georgian." *Lingua* 26: 291-301.

Bailey, Charles-James. 1973. "The Patterning of Language Variation." In *Varieties of Present-Day English*. Ed. by R. Bailey
and J. Robinson, pp. 156-186. New York: The Macmillan Co.

Bech, Gunnar. 1969. "Über die gotischen Gen. Pl.-Engungen."
Lingua 23: 55-64.

Benveniste, Emile. 1935. *Origines de la formation des noms en
indoeuropéen*. Paris: Librairie Adrien-Maisonneuve.

—————. 1971. "Toward an Analysis of Case Functions: The
Latin Genitive." In *Problems in General Linguistics*. Trans. by
N. Meek, pp. 121-127. Coral Gables: University of Miami Press.

Biese, Y. M. 1950. "Some Notes on the Origin of the Indo-European
Nominative Singular." *Annales Academiae Scientiarum Fennicae*.
Series B. Vol. 63, No. 5.

Blümel, Wolfgang. 1972. *Untersuchungen zu Lautsystem und Morphologie des vorklassischen Lateins*. *Münchener Studien zur Sprachwissenschaft Beihaft* 8, Neue Folge. München: R. Kitzinger.

Brosman, Paul. 1976. "The Hittite Gender of Cognates of PIE
Feminines." *The Journal of Indo-European Studies* 4: 141-159.

—————. 1978. "The Hittite Gender of Cognates of PIE Neuters."
The Journal of Indo-European Studies 6: 93-106.

Brugmann, Karl. 1891. *Elements of the Comparative Grammar of the
Indo-Germanic Languages*. Vol. 2. Trans. by R. Conway and W.
Rouse. London: Karl J. Trübner.

Brugmann, Karl. 1893. *Elements of the Comparative Grammar of the Indo-Germanic Languages.* Vol. 3. Trans. by R. Conway and W. Rouse. London: Karl J. Trübner.

——————. 1897. *The Nature and Origin of the Noun Genders in the Indo-European Languages.* Trans. by E. Robbins. New York: Charles Schribner's Sons.

——————. 1904. *Kurze vergleichende Grammatik der indogermanischen Sprachen.* Strassburg: Karl J. Trübner.

——————. 1911. *Grundriss der vergleichenden Grammatik der indogermanischen Sprachen.* Vol. 2.2. Strassburg: Karl J. Trübner.

——————. 1916. *Grundriss der vergleichenden Grammatik der indogermanischen Sprachen.* Vol. 2.3. Strassburg: Karl J. Trübner.

——————. 1930. *Grundriss der vergleichenden Grammatik der indogermanischen Sprachen.* Vol. 1.2. Berlin: Walter de Gruyter.

Buck, Carl. 1933. *Comparative Grammar of Greek and Latin.* Chicago: University of Chicago Press.

Burrow, T. 1949. "'Schwa' in Sanskrit." *Transactions of the Philological Society.* 22-61.

——————. 1973. *The Sanskrit Language.* Rev. ed. London: Faber and Faber.

——————. 1979. *The Problem of Schwa in Sanskrit.* Oxford: Oxford University Press.

Chen, Matthew and William S-Y Wang. 1975. "Sound Change: Actuation and Implementation." *Language* 51: 255-281.

Chomsky, Noam and Morris Halle. 1968. *The Sound Pattern of English.* New York: Harper and Row.

Clark, Eve. 1978. "'Locationals: Existential, Locative, and Possessive Constructions." In *Universals of Human Language.* Vol. 4. Ed. by J. Greenberg, pp. 85-126. Stanford: Stanford University Press.

Coleman, Robert. 1972. "Review of *The Latin Thematic Genitive,* by Andrew MacKay Devine." *Lingua* 30: 72-78.

Comrie, Bernard. 1978. "Ergativity." In *Syntactic Typology.* Ed. by W. Lehmann, pp. 329-394. Austin: University of Texas Press.

Conway, R. Seymour. 1889. "Grammatical Gender." *The Classical Review* 3: 469.

Cowgill, Warren. 1970. "The Nominative Plural and Preterit Singular of the Active Participles in Baltic." In *Baltic Linguistics.* Ed. by T. Magner and W. Schmalstieg, pp. 23-37. University Park: The Pennsylvania State University Press.

Cruse, D. A. 1973. "Some Thoughts on Agentivity." *Journal of Linguistics* 9: 11-23.

Dixon, R. M. W. 1972. *The Dyirbal Language of North Queensland.* Cambridge: Cambridge University Press.

——————. 1979. "Ergativity." *Language* 55: 59-138.

Dyen, Isidore. 1974. "Genetic Classification and Affix Reconstruction: The PIE Ending of the Genitive Singular of *O*-Stem Nouns." In *Historical Linguistics II: Theory and Description in Phonology.* Ed. by J. Anderson and C. Jones, pp. 123-139. Amsterdam: North-Holland.

Endzelīns, J. 1944. *Altpreussische Grammatik.* Rīga: Latvju Gramata.

——————. 1971. *Comparative Phonology and Morphology of the Baltic Languages.* Trans. by W. Schmalstieg and B. Jēgers. The Hague: Mouton.

Erhart, Adolf. 1967. "Zur ie. Nominalflexion." *Sborník Prací Filosofické Fakulty Brněnské University.* 7-26.

——————. 1970. *Studien zur indoeuropäischen Morphologie.* Brno: Opera Universitatis Purkynianae Brunensis Facultas Philosophica.

Fillmore, Charles. 1968. "The Case for Case." In *Universals in Linguistic Theory.* Ed. by E. Bach and R. Harms, pp. 1-88. New York: Holt, Rinehart and Winston.

Flobert, Pierre. 1975. *Les verbes déponents latins: des origines à Charlemagne.* Paris: Société d'Edition 'Les Belles Lettres'.

Fodor, Istvan. 1959. "The Origin of Grammatical Gender." *Lingua* 8: 1-41, 186-214.

Fowler, Murray. 1957. "Review of *The Character of the Indo-European Moods, with Special Regard to Greek and Sanskrit,* by J. Gonda." *Language* 33: 50-54.

Friedrich, Johannes. 1974. *Hethitisches Elementarbuch I.* 2nd ed. Heidelberg: Carl Winter.

Frisk, Hjalmer. 1970. *Griechisches etymologisches Wörterbuch.* Vol. 1. Heidelberg: Carl Winter.

Gimbutas, Marija. 1970. "Proto-Indo-European Culture: The Kurgan Culture during the Fifth, Fourth, and Third Millennia B.C." In *Indo-European and Indo-Europeans.* Ed. by G. Cardona, H. Hoenigswald, and A. Senn, pp. 155-197. Philadelphia: University of Pennsylvania Press.

——————. 1973. "Old Europe c. 7000-3500 B.C.: The Earliest European Civilization before the Infiltration of the Indo-European Peoples." *The Journal of Indo-European Studies* 1: 1-20.

——————. 1974. "An Archaeologist's View of PIE in 1975." *The Journal of Indo-European Studies* 2: 289-307.

Godel, Robert. 1975. *An Introduction to the Study of Classical Armenian.* Wiesbaden: Dr. Ludwig Reichert Verlag.

Golab, Zbigniew. 1969. "Subject as a Linguistic Category." *General Linguistics* 9. 1-12.

Gonda, J. 1956. *The Character of the Indo-European Moods, with Special Regard to Greek and Sanskrit.* Wiesbaden: Otto Harrassowitz.

Gray, Louis. 1932. "On Indo-European Noun-Declension, Especially of *-O-* and *-Ā-* Stems." *Language* 8: 183-199.

Guild, David. 1970. "The Development of the Concept of Definiteness in Baltic and Slavic." In *Donum Balticum.* Ed. by V. Rūķe-Draviņa, pp. 162-172. Stockholm: Almqvist and Wiksell.

Hartmann, Hans. 1954. *Das Passiv: eine Studie zur Geistesgeschichte der Kelten, Italiker, und Arier.* Heidelberg: Carl Winter.

Hirt, Hermann, 1927. *Indogermanische Grammatik.* Vol. 3. Heidelberg: Carl Winter.

——————. 1932. *Handbuch des Urgermanischen.* Vol. 3. Heidelberg: Carl Winter.

——————. 1934. *Indogermanische Grammatik.* Vol. 6. Heidelberg: Carl Winter.

Hockett, Charles. 1957. "Problems of Morphemic Analysis." In *Readings in Linguistics.* Vol. 1. Ed. by M. Joos, pp. 229-242. Chicago: University of Chicago Press.

Houwink ten Cate, Philo. 1967. "The Ending *-d* of the Hittite Possessive Pronoun." *Revue Hittite et Asianique* 24: 123-132.

Ivanov, V. 1958. "The Importance of New Data Concerning Hittite and Tocharian Languages for the Comparative Historical Grammar of Indo-European Languages." In *Proceedings of the Eighth Congress of Linguists*. Ed. by E. Sivertsen, pp. 611-614. Oslo: Oslo University Press.

Jasanoff, Jay. 1973. "The Hittite Ablative in *-anz(a)*." *Münchener Studien zur Sprachwissenschaft* 31: 123-128.

Jeffers, Robert. 1976. "Review of *Proto-Indo-European Syntax*, by Winfred P. Lehmann." *Language* 52: 982-988.

Jespersen, Otto. 1935. *The Philosophy of Grammar*. London: George Allen and Unwin.

Josephson, F. 1967. "Pronominal Adverbs of Anatolian: Formation and Function." *Revue Hittite et Asianique* 24: 133-154.

Kammenhuber, Annelies. 1979. "Direktiv, Terminativ und/oder Lokativ im Hethitischen." In *Hethitisch und Indogermanisch*. Ed. by E. Neu and W. Meid, pp. 115-142. *Innsbrucker Beiträge zur Sprachwissenschaft* 25. Innsbruck: Institut für Sprachwissenschaft der Universität Innsbruck.

King, Robert. 1969. *Historical Linguistics and Generative Grammar*. Englewood Cliffs: Prentice-Hall.

Knobloch, Jean. 1954. "La voyelle thématique *-e-/-o-* serait-elle un indice d'objet indo-européen?" *Lingua* 3: 407-420.

Krause, Wolfgang and Werner Thomas. 1960. *Tocharisches Elementarbuch*. Vol. 1. Heidelberg: Carl Winter.

Kronasser, Heinz. 1956. *Vergleichende Laut- und Formenlehre des Hethitischen*. Heidelberg: Carl Winter.

——————. 1966. *Etymologie der hethitischen Sprache*. Wiesbaden: Otto Harrassowitz.

Kurylowicz, Jerzy. 1958. "Le hittite: rapport par J. Kurylowicz." In *Proceedings of the Eighth Congress of Linguists*. Ed. by E. Sivertsen, pp. 216-251. Oslo: Oslo University Press.

——————. 1964. *The Inflectional Categories of Indo-European*. Heidelberg: Carl Winter.

Labov, William. 1972. "The Internal Evolution of Linguistic Rules." In *Linguistic Change and Generative Theory*. Ed. by R. Stockwell and R. Macaulay, pp. 101-171. Bloomington: Indiana University Press.

Lane, George. 1951. "Review of *Objektive Konjugation im Indogermanischen*, by Paul Kretschmer, and *Some Notes on the Origin of the Indo-European Nominative Singular*, by Y. M. Biese." *Language* 27: 370-374.

——————. 1961. "On the Formation of the Indo-European Demonstrative." *Language* 37: 469-475.

Lehmann, Winfred. 1958. "On Earlier Stages of the Indo-European Nominal Inflection." *Language* 34: 179-202.

——————. 1967. "The Gothic Genitive Plural *-ē*: Focus of Exercises in Theory." In *Papers in Honor of Leon Dostert*. Ed. by W. Austin, pp. 108-111. The Hague: Mouton.

——————. 1970. "Definite Adjective Declensions and Syntactic Types." In *Donum Balticum*. Ed. by V. Rūķe-Draviņa, pp. 286-290. Stockholm: Almqvist and Wiksell.

——————. 1973. *Historical Linguistics: An Introduction*. 2nd ed. New York: Holt, Rinehart and Winston.

——————. 1974. *Proto-Indo-European Syntax*. Austin: University of Texas Press.

Malkiel, Yakov. 1957. "Diachronic Hypercharacterization in Romance." *Archivum Linguisticum* 9.2: 79-113 and 9.3: 1-36.

Mańczak, Withold. 1958. "Tendances générales des changements analogiques." *Lingua* 7: 298-325, 387-420.

Mann, Stuart. 1968. *An Armenian Historical Grammar in Latin Characters*. London: Luzac and Co.

Markey, T. L. 1979. "Deixis and the *u*-Perfect." *The Journal of Indo-European Studies* 7: 65-75.

Martinet, André. 1957. "Le genre féminin en indo-européen: examen fonctionnel du probleme." *Bulletin de la société de linguistique de Paris* 52: 83-95.

—————. 1962. *A Functional View of Language*. London: Oxford University Press.

Marvan, Jiří. 1973a. "Baltic and Indo-European Ergative." *Lituanus* 19: 31-38.

—————. 1973b. "Deciphering the Old Prussian 'Message'." In *Baltic Literature and Linguistics*. Ed. by A. Ziedonis, J. Puhvel, R. Silbajoris, and M. Valgemaë, pp. 181-188. Columbus: Association for the Advancement of Baltic Studies, Ohio State University.

Matthews, P. H. 1974. *Morphology: An Introduction to the Theory of Word-Structure*. Cambridge: Cambridge University Press.

Meillet, A. 1931. "Essai de chronologie des langues indo-européennes." *Bulletin de la société de linguistique de Paris* 32: 1-28.

—————. 1964. *Introduction à l'étude comparative des langues indo-européenes*. University, Alabama: University of Alabama Press.

—————. 1970. *General Characteristics of the Germanic Languages*. Trans. by W. Dismukes. Coral Gables: University of Miami Press.

Meillet, A. and Marcel Cohen, eds. 1952. *Les langues du monde*. New ed. Paris: Champion.

Miranda, Rocky. 1975. "Indo-European Gender: A Study in Semantic and Syntactic Change." *The Journal of Indo-European Studies* 3: 199-215.

Must, Gustav. 1952. "The Gothic Genitive Plural in *-ē*." *Language* 28: 218-221.

Neu, Erich. 1969. "Review of *Die griechischen Adjektive zweier Endungen auf -OS*, by Wolfgang Kastner." *Indogermanische Forschungen* 74: 235-241.

—————. 1979. "Einige Überlegungen zu den hethitischen Kasusendungen." In *Hethitisch und Indogermanisch*. Ed. by E. Neu and W. Meid, pp. 177-196. *Innsbrucker Beiträge zur Sprachwissenschaft* 25. Innsbruck: Institut für Sprachwissenschaft der Universität Innsbruck.

Pajares, Alberto Bernabé. 1976. "A Critical Review of Some Interpretations of the IE Long Diphthongs (I)." *Archivum Linguisticum* 7: 161-190.

Parmenter, C., S. Treviño and C. Bevans. 1933. "The Influence of a Change in Pitch on the Articulation of a Vowel." *Language* 9: 72-81.

Pei, Mario. 1966. *Glossary of Linguistic Terminology*. New York: Columbia University Press.

Perrot, Jean. 1961. *Les dérivés latins en -men et -mentum*. Paris: Librairie C. Klincksieck.

Petersen, Walter. 1932. "The Inflection of Indo-European Personal Pronouns." *Language* 8: 164-193.

—————. 1939. "The Primary Cases of the Tocharian Nominal Declension." *Language* 15: 72-98.

Poultney, James. 1967. "Some Indo-European Morphological Alternations." *Language* 43: 871-882.

Prokosch, E. 1939. *A Comparative Germanic Grammar*. Baltimore:
Linguistic Society of America.

Pulgram, Ernst. 1959. "Proto-Indo-European Reality and Reconstruction." *Language* 35: 421-426.

——————. 1961. "The Nature and Use of Proto-Languages." *Lingua*
10: 18-37.

Reighard, John. 1974. "Variable Rules in Historical Linguistics."
In *Historical Linguistics I: Syntax, Morphology, Internal and
Comparative Reconstruction*. Ed. by J. Anderson and C. Jones, pp.
252-262. Amsterdam: North-Holland.

Rosenkranz, B. 1949. "Das griechische Adverbium auf -ōs." *Zeitschrift für vergleichende Sprachforschung* 63: 241-249.

Safarewicz, Jan. 1974. *Linguistic Studies*. The Hague: Mouton.

Savčenko, A. N. 1967. "Èrgativnaja konstrukcija predloženija v
praindoevropejskom jazyke." In *Èrgativnaja konstrukcija predloženija v jazykax različnyx tipov*. Ed. by V. Žirmuskij, pp. 74-90.
Leningrad: Nauka.

Schane, Sanford. 1976. "The Best Argument Is in the Mind of the
Beholder." In *Assessing Linguistic Arguments*. Ed. by J. Wirth,
pp. 167-185. Washington, D.C.: Hemisphere Publishing Corporation.

Schindler, Jochem. 1975. "The Ablaut of the Indo-European *R/N*
Stems." In *Indo-European Studies*. Vol. 2. Ed. by C. Watkins,
pp. 211-225. Cambridge, Mass.: Department of Linguistics, Harvard University.

Schmalstieg, William. 1971. "Die Entwicklung der ā-Deklination im
Slavischen." *Zeitschrift für slavische Philologie* 36: 130-146.

——————. 1973. "New Thoughts on Indo-European Phonology."
Zeitschrift für vergleichende Sprachforschung 87: 99-157.

——————. 1974a. *An Old Prussian Grammar*. University Park: The
Pennsylvania State University Press.

——————. 1974b. "Dual and Plural." Unpublished.

——————. 1974c. "Some Morphological Implications of the Indo-
European Passage of *-oN to *-ō." *Zeitschrift für vergleichende
Sprachforschung* 88: 187-198.

——————. 1975. "The Baltic First Person Singular Ending -u."
General Linguistics 15: 168-175.

——————. 1976a. *An Introduction to Old Church Slavic*. Cambridge,
Mass.: Slavica Press.

——————. 1976b. "Speculations on the Indo-European Active and
Middle Voices." *Zeitschrift für vergleichende Sprachforschung* 90:
23-36.

——————. 1977a. "A Note on Tokharian B Verbs of the Type
palkau." *Orbis* 26: 293-296.

——————. 1977b. "Speculations on the Development of the Indo-
European Nominal Inflection." *Folia Linguistica* 10: 109-149.

——————. 1978. "More on Indo-European Monophthongizations: A
Reply to Dr. Alberto Bernabé-Pajares." *Archivum Linguisticum* 9:
135-162.

——————. 1980. *Indo-European Linguistics: A New Synthesis*.
University Park: The Pennsylvania State University Press.

Schmid, Wolfgang. 1973. "Sprachwissenschaftliche Bemerkungen zum
hethitischen 'Direktiv'." In *Festschrift Heinrich Otten*. Ed. by
E. Neu and C. Rüster, pp. 291-301. Wiesbaden: Otto Harrassowitz.

Schmidt, Gernot. 1978. *Stammbildung und Flexion der indogerman-ischen Personalpronomina.* Wiesbaden: Otto Harrassowitz.

Schmidt, Johannes. 1889. *Die Pluralbildungen der indogermanischen Neutra.* Weimar: Hermann Böhlau.

Schmidt, Karl H. 1979. "Reconstructing Active and Ergative Stages of Pre-Indo-European." In *Ergativity: Towards a Theory of Gram-matical Relations.* Ed. by F. Plant, pp. 333-345. London: Academic Press.

Schuchardt, H. 1905/06. "Über den aktivischen und passivischen Charakter des Transitivs." *Indogermanische Forschungen* 18: 528-531.

Seebold, Elmar. 1971. "Versuch über die Herkunft der indogerman-ischen Personalendungs-System." *Zeitschrift für vergleichende Sprachforschung* 95: 185-210.

Shields, Kenneth. 1976. "On the Origin of Normal Reduplication in Indo-European. *Orbis* 25: 37-43.

——————. 1977. "Evidence of I.E. *-bhi in Tocharian." *Folia Linguistica* 11: 281-286.

——————. 1978a. "A Note on I.E. *-tōt." *The Journal of Indo-European Studies* 6: 133-140.

——————. 1978b. "Some Remarks Concerning Early Indo-European Nominal Inflection." *The Journal of Indo-European Studies* 6: 185-210.

——————. 1978c. "Speculations Concerning the I.E. Root *es-." *Archivum Linguisticum* 9: 73-78.

——————. 1979a. "A Theory of Gender Change." *Glossa* 13: 27-38.

——————. 1979b. "IE */b/ and the Theory of Lexical Diffusion." *Linguistics* 17: 709-714.

——————. 1979c. "More on Early Indo-European Nominal Inflection: The Origin of the -R-/-N-Stems." *The Journal of Indo-European Studies* 7: 213-226.

——————. 1979d. "On the Indo-European Primary Verbal Suffix *-ye/o-." *Euroasiatica* 4.4: 7-16.

——————. 1980a. "Fast Speech and the Origin of the Standard English Verbal Suffix -s." *Journal of English Linguistics* 14: 24-35.

——————. 1980b. "Sociolinguistics and the Reconstruction of Proto-Indo-European." *Anthropological Linguistics* 22: 225-232.

——————. 1980c. "The Oscan-Umbrian Third Person Plural Secondary Verbal Ending -ns." *Glotta* 58: 68-77.

——————. 1980d. "The Sanskrit Aorist Passive." *Indian Linguis-tics* 41: 31-36.

——————. Forthcoming a. "Some Remarks about the I.E. Compara-tive." *Orbis.*

——————. Forthcoming b. "Speculations about the Early Indo-European Verb." *Word.*

Sihler, Andrew. 1977. "Loss of *w and *y in Vedic Sanskrit." *Indo-Iranian Journal* 19: 5-20.

Specht, Franz. 1947. *Der Ursprung der indogermanischen Deklination.* Göttingen: Vandenhoeck and Ruprecht.

Stang, Christian. 1966. *Vergleichende Grammatik der baltischen Sprachen.* Oslo: Universitetsforlaget.

Starke, Frank. 1977. *Die Funktionen der dimensionalen Kasus und Adverbien im Althethitischen. Studien zu den Boğazköy-Texten* 23. Wiesbaden: Otto Harrassowitz.

Strang, Barbara. 1970. *A History of English.* London: Methuen and Co.

Sturtevant, E. H. 1925. "Remarks on the Lydian Inscriptions." *Language* 1: 69-79.

—————. 1932. "The Ablative in Indo-European and Hittite." *Language* 8: 1-10.

—————. 1933. *A Comparative Grammar of the Hittite Language.* Philadelphia: Linguistic Society of America.

—————. 1951. *A Comparative Grammar of the Hittite Language.* Rev. ed. New Haven: Yale University Press.

Szemerényi, Oswald. 1956. "Hittite Pronominal Inflection and the Development of Syllabic Liquids and Nasals." *Zeitschrift für vergleichende Sprachforschung* 73: 57-80.

—————. 1970. *Einführung in die vergleichende Sprachwissenschaft.* Darmstadt: Wissenschaftliche Buchgesellschaft.

Tchekhoff, Claude. 1978. "Le double cas-sujet des inanimés: un archaïsme de la syntaxe hittite?" *Bulletin de la société de linguistique de Paris* 73: 225-241.

Thumb, Albert and Richard Hauschild. 1959. *Handbuch des Sanskrit.* Pt. 2. 3rd ed. Heidelberg: Carl Winter.

Thurneysen, R. 1946. *A Grammar of Old Irish.* Trans. by D. Binchy and O. Bergin. Dublin: Institute for Advanced Studies.

Twadell, W. F. 1948. "The Prehistoric Germanic Short Syllabics." *Language* 24: 139-151.

Uhlenbeck, C. D. 1901. "Agens und Patiens im Kasussystem der indogermanischen Sprachen." *Indogermanische Forschungen* 12: 170-171.

Vaillant, André. 1936. "L'ergatif indo-européen." *Bulletin de la société de linguistique de Paris* 37: 93-108.

Wackernagel, Jacob and Albert Debrunner. 1896. *Altindische Grammatik.* Vol. 1. Göttingen: Vandenhoeck and Ruprecht.

—————. 1930. *Altindische Grammatik.* Vol. 3. Göttingen: Vandenhoeck and Ruprecht.

Wakelin, Martyn. 1974. "New Light on IE *R/N* Stems in Germanic?" *Studia Linguistica* 28: 109-111.

Wandruszka, Mario. 1969. "Polymorphie und Polysemie." In *Festschrift für Hugo Moser.* Ed. by U. Engel, P. Grebe, and H. Rupp, pp. 218-232. Düsseldorf: Pädagogischer Verlag Schwann.

Wang, William. 1969. "Competing Changes as a Cause of Residue." *Language* 45: 9-25.

Watkins, Calvert. 1962. *Indo-European Origins of the Celtic Verb.* Dublin: Institute for Advanced Studies.

—————. 1967. "Italo-Celtic Revisited." In *Ancient Indo-European Dialects.* Ed. by H. Birnbaum and J. Puhvel, pp. 29-50. Berkeley: University of California Press.

—————. 1969. *Indogermanische Grammatik: Geschichte der indogermanische Verbalflexion.* Vol. 3, Pt. 1. Heidelberg: Carl Winter.

Weinreich, Uriel, William Labov and Marvin Herzog. 1968. "Empirical Foundations for a Theory of Language Change." In *Directions for Historical Linguistics.* Ed. by W. Lehmann and Y. Malkiel, pp. 95-195. Austin: University of Texas Press.

Wheeler, Benjamin. 1898. "The Origin of Grammatical Gender."
Journal of English and German Philology 2: 528-545.

Whitney, William D. 1973. *Sanskrit Grammar*. 2nd ed. Cambridge,
Mass.: Harvard University Press.

Wright, Joseph and O. L. Sayce. 1968. *Grammar of the Gothic Language*. 2nd ed. Oxford: Clarendon Press.

Wyatt, William. 1970. *Indo-European /a/*. Philadelphia: University
of Pennsylvania Press.

──────────. 1972. "Review of *Geschichte der indogermanische Verbalflexion*, by Calvert Watkins." *Language* 48: 687-695.